The McKinsey *Quarterly*

On the cove

D1314157

The crisis: A new era in management

Strategy

Strategy/By Invitation

Leading through uncertainty

Lowell Bryan
and Diana Farrell

24

When Lehman Brothers failed in September 2008, it touched off a chain of events that left senior executives confronting a more profoundly uncertain business environment than most of them have ever faced.

Uncertainty pervades not only the downturn's depth and duration but also the very future of the global economic order.

In an environment like this, companies must evaluate an unusually broad set of macroeconomic outcomes and strategic responses and then act to make themselves more flexible, aware, and resilient.

The payoff for companies that take these steps will go beyond mere survival; if history is any guide, today's uncertainty will also give rise to extraordinary opportunity.

Strategy in a 'structural break'

Richard P. Rumelt

35

A structural break with the past often means hard times. Adjustment is neither easy nor quick, and some organizations don't survive.

Yet others prosper because old patterns are swept away and new ones emerge. The first order of the day is to endure, but the second is to exploit the new forces.

In a very real sense, a structural break is the best time to be a strategist. At the moment of change, old sources of advantage weaken and new ones appear. Afterward, upstarts can leap ahead of seemingly entrenched players.

On the cover

The crisis: A new era in management

Strategy

Marketing

Corporate Finance

Feature articles

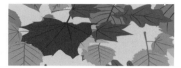

Departments

On our Web site

Now available on mckinseyquarterly.com

New on climate change

Strategy

Seven ways China might surprise us in 2009

The country could yet again change the way the world sees it. Here's a shortlist of realistic possibilities.

Health care

The missed opportunity for US health insurers

At present, most health care payers convert less than 10 percent of the customers who move to a new product class. There's substantial room for improvement.

High Tech

Rethinking high-tech distribution

Distributors may hold the key to high-tech sales growth in many markets.

Information Technology

Data centers: How to cut carbon emissions *and* costs

The demand for data center capacity worldwide has led to a sharp rise in IT costs and a steady increase in carbon emissions. A new efficiency metric provides companies with a clear yardstick for measuring progress.

Corporate Finance

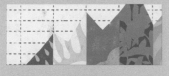

How climate change could affect corporate valuations

Efforts to reduce climate change can profoundly affect the valuations of many companies, but executives so far seem largely unaware.

Strategy

Helping 'green' products grow

When customers reach the cash register, they often forget their eco-friendly attitudes. Businesses can do a lot more to help would-be "green" consumers walk their talk.

Strategy

Lessons from innovation's front lines: An interview with IDEO's CEO

Tim Brown, whose company specializes in innovation, distills the lessons of his career.

Governance

Turning around a struggling airline: An interview with the CEO of Malaysia Airlines

Idris Jala led the state-controlled carrier from the brink of bankruptcy to record-breaking profits. Now he wants it to become what he calls a "five-star value carrier."

Corporate Finance

Better communications for better investors: An interview with the CFO of Gartner

Gartner CFO Christopher Lafond discusses the company's assertive approach to managing relationships with investors.

Surveys

Economic conditions snapshot, December 2008: McKinsey Global Survey Results

A survey in the field from December 2 to December 8 describes a tough month. Compared with one month earlier, twice as many executives now expect their companies' profit to fall in 2009, and more than half expect deflation in their countries in the first quarter. Small, private companies are still doing better than others.

Assessing innovation metrics: McKinsey Global Survey Results

A recent McKinsey Global Survey shows that companies are satisfied, overall, with their use of metrics to assess innovation portfolios—though many findings suggest that they shouldn't be. The companies that get the highest returns from innovation do use metrics well; these organizations tend to assess innovation more comprehensively than the others.

More from mckinseyquarterly.com

Experience multimedia

View our videos
Visit our Web site for new videos on important topics and interviews with executives.

mckinseyquarterly.com/video

Recently added videos:

Klaus Kleinfeld on the global downturn

Alcoa's CEO sees risks in antibusiness rhetoric, but also a chance for speedier recovery.

Warming to the opportunities of climate change

Businesses are beginning to embrace the economics of carbon reduction.

Explore our interactives
Take the information further: watch and learn from our interactive presentations.

mckinseyquarterly.com/interactive

Recently added interactives:

Value creation in health care: A sector-by-sector analysis

Success is not just about top-line growth.

Carbon capture and storage

Executives and public policy makers should familiarize themselves with the technologies involved in carbon capture and storage (CCS) as they work toward reducing CO_2 levels in the atmosphere.

Put our widget on your page
Our widget allows you to view, read, and share *Quarterly* content on your social network, blog, or personalized page.

Join the conversation

These short essays by leading thinkers in their field, within and outside of McKinsey, are designed to encourage discussion. Read what people are saying, and then join the conversation.

Recent conversation starters:

Andy Grove's electric crusade

The legendary former CEO of Intel explains why he has become a passionate advocate for retrofitting America's car fleet to go electric—and for rebuilding the domestic battery industry. Read his plan, and then tell us what you think.

Nurturing entrepreneurship in India's villages

The world's great cities and the professionals who live in them are linked more tightly to one another than they are with their own rural hinterlands. Yet true prosperity starts in the countryside. In this article, Professor Tarun Khanna of Harvard Business School discusses how India must invest in its rural economy if the country is to be a competitive global player.

This Quarter

A time for leadership

These are no ordinary times. The venerable independent investment banks Lehman Brothers and Bear Stearns no longer exist. Central bankers and finance ministers, working in concert, are battling to keep up with events. China's government is pumping hundreds of billions of dollars into the country's economy. Chief executives in the US financial-services and automotive sectors have gone to Washington, hats in hand.

Along the way, many core assumptions about the merits of globalization, markets, risk, and debt—long taken for granted in business, government, and academia—have come into question. One big shift already under way involves a far larger economic role for government, whether through outright ownership of former private-sector assets or tighter regulation. Also inevitable: massive changes in industry structures. Consolidation, effected either by bankruptcy or merger, is already transforming financial services and seems bound to take place elsewhere as the impact of the credit crisis ripples through the real economy.

The cover package in this issue of the *Quarterly* focuses on the managerial implications of the economic transition that has just begun. A critical theme running through much of the content, starting with "Leading through uncertainty," by Lowell Bryan and Diana Farrell, is how to cope with the extraordinary uncertainty permeating today's business environment. To set strategy, companies must not only consider an unusually broad range of potential outcomes but also grapple with the implications of a downturn that represents a "structural break," as Professor Richard P. Rumelt terms it in his essay. We have also distilled practical advice for executives on issues— managing costs, obtaining financing, working with regulators, adjusting sales and marketing—that are more pressing and require fresher thinking than they did in past downturns.

I wish to close with a few words on leadership, which is sorely needed on the international level to renew the global financial system and avert a backlash of protectionism or excessive regulation that could derail economic progress— especially in countries and regions emerging from poverty—or dampen the entrepreneurial spirit. Within organizations, strong leadership is equally critical. Anxious employees, customers, suppliers, and shareholders are looking for a steady hand and clear, candid messages from corporate leaders, not for unrealistic pronouncements that may be overtaken by next week's events. The world is watching.

Ian Davis

Ian Davis
Managing director, McKinsey & Company

In Brief

Research and perspectives on management

Using **'power curves'** to assess industry dynamics

Michele Zanini

Major crises and downturns often produce shakeouts that redefine industry structures. However, these crises do not fundamentally change an underlying structural trend: the increasing inequality in the size and performance of large companies. Indeed, a financial crisis—for example, the one that erupted in 2008—is likely to accelerate this intriguing long-term tendency.

The past decade has seen the rise of many "mega-institutions"—companies of unprecedented scale and scope—that have steadily pulled away from their smaller competitors.[1] What has received less attention is the striking degree of inequality in the size and performance of even the mega-institutions themselves. Plotting the distribution of net income among the global top 150 corporations in 2005, for example, doesn't yield a common bell curve, which would imply a relatively even spread of values around a mean. The result instead is a "power curve," which, unlike normal distributions, implies that most companies are below average.

Such a curve is characterized by a short "head," comprising a small set of companies with extremely large incomes, and drops off quickly to a long "tail" of companies with significantly smaller incomes. This pattern, similar to those illustrating the distribution of wealth among ultrarich individuals, is described by a mathematical relationship called a "power law."[2] The relationship is simple: a variable (for example, net income) is a function of another variable (for example, rank by net income) with an exponent (for example, rank raised to a power).

Exhibit 1 shows the top 30 US banks and savings institutions in June 1994, 2007, and 2008, measured by their domestic deposits (the 2008 shares of different institutions were adjusted to reflect the surge of banking M&A in the autumn of 2008). The exhibit shows that inequality has been increasing from 1994 (when the number-ten bank was roughly 30 percent of the size of the largest one) to 2008 (when it was only 10 percent as large as the first-ranked institution). It also shows how in 2008, the financial crisis accelerated the growth of the top five compared with the other banks in the top

ten as the largest financial institutions took advantage of their relatively healthy balance sheets and absorbed banks in the next tier. Regulation could put a damper on this crisis-driven acceleration of inequality, but power curve dynamics suggest that it will not reverse the trend. Indeed, we found long-term patterns of increasing inequality in size and performance in a variety of industries and markets when we used metrics such as market value, revenues, income, and assets to plot the size of companies by rank.

Our analysis suggests that an industry's degree of openness and competitive intensity is an important determinant of its power curve dynamics. You would expect a bigger number of competitors and consumer choices to flatten the curve, but in fact the larger the system, the larger the gap between the number-one and

EXHIBIT I

Increasing inequality in banking

Top 30 US commercial banks and savings institutions by total domestic deposits; index: largest company = 100

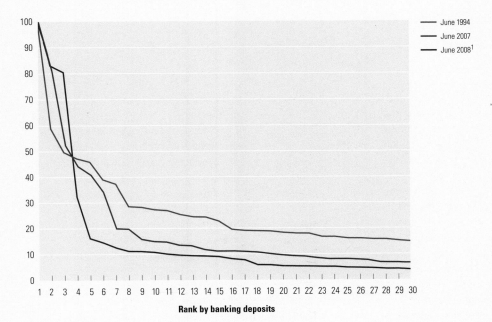

Rank by banking deposits

— June 1994
— June 2007
— June 2008[1]

[1] Adjusted to reflect acquisitions from June to Oct 2008.

Source: FDIC; McKinsey analysis

the median spot. As Exhibit 1 shows, after the liberalization of US interstate banking, in 1994, deposits grew significantly faster in the top-ranking banks than in the lower-ranking ones, creating a steeper power curve. Greater openness may create a more level playing field at first, but progressively greater differentiation and consolidation tend to occur over time, as they did when the United States liberalized its telecom market.

Power curves are also promoted by intangible assets—talent, networks, brands, and intellectual property—because they can drive increasing returns to scale, generate economies of scope, and help differentiate value propositions. Exhibit 2 shows a significant degree of inequality, across the board, in the size and performance of companies in a number of sectors we researched. But the more labor- or capital-intensive sectors, such as chemicals and machinery, have flatter curves than intangible-rich ones, such as software and biotech.

The fact that industry structures and outcomes appear to be distributed around "natural" values opens up an intriguing new field of research into the strategic implications. Notably, the extreme outcomes that characterize power curves suggest that strategic thrusts rather than incremental strategies are required to improve a company's position significantly. Consider the retail mutual-fund industry, for example. The major players sitting atop this power curve (Exhibit 3) have opportunities to extend their lead over smaller players by exploiting network effects, such as cross-selling individual retirement accounts (IRAs), to a large installed base of 401(k) plan holders as they roll over their assets. The financial crisis of 2008 may well boost this opportunity further as weakened financial institutions consider placing their asset-management units on the block to raise capital.

When executives set strategy, power curves can be a useful diagnostic tool for understanding an industry's structural

EXHIBIT 2

Sector variations

Distribution of market values, 2006; index: company with highest market value in each sector = 100

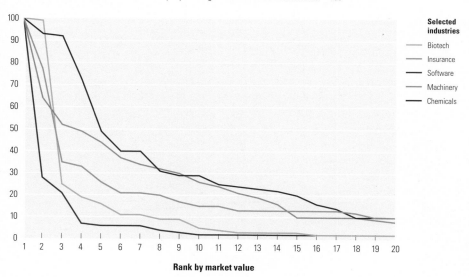

Selected industries
— Biotech
— Insurance
— Software
— Machinery
— Chemicals

Rank by market value

Source: Global Vantage; McKinsey analysis

EXHIBIT 3

A steep slope

US 401(k) assets under management by top 30 companies, 2006, $ billion

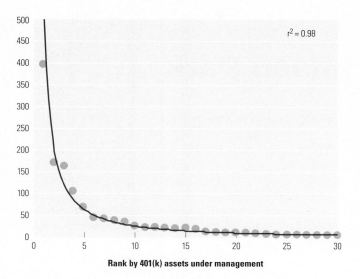

$r^2 = 0.98$

Rank by 401(k) assets under management

---

r^2 is the proportion of variance explained by a regression.

Source: Pensions & Investments; McKinsey analysis

dynamics. In particular, there may well be commonalities across sectors in the way these curves evolve, and that might make it possible to gain better insights—based on the experience of other industries—into an industry's evolution. As the importance of intangible assets increases across sectors, for example, will power curves in media and insurance resemble the currently much steeper ones found in today's intangible-rich sectors such as software and biotech? Power curves could also benchmark an industry's performance. Curves for specific industries evolve over many years, so the appearance of large deviations from a more recent "norm" can indicate exceptional performance, on one hand, or instability in the market, on the other.

Unlike the laws of physics, power curves aren't immutable. But their ubiquity and consistency suggest that companies are generally competing not only against one another but also against an industry structure that becomes progressively more unequal. For most companies, this possibility makes power curves an important piece of the strategic context. Senior executives must understand them and respect their implications.

Michele Zanini is an associate principal in McKinsey's Boston office.

[1] See Lowell L. Bryan and Michele Zanini, "Strategy in an era of global giants," mckinseyquarterly.com, November 2005.
[2] The power laws phenomenon has been explored in the recent books *The Black Swan: The Impact of the Highly Improbable* (Nassim Nicholas Taleb, Random House, 2007) and *The Long Tail: Why the Future of Business is Selling Less of More* (Chris Anderson, Hyperion, 2006).

Visit this article online at mckinseyquarterly.com for reader responses.

Speaking of Organization

An interview with
Yongmaan Park

Dominic Barton and Clayton G. Deutsch

In the mid-1990s, South Korea's Doosan was a century-old consumer goods conglomerate struggling under a cash flow crisis and facing new competition. Over the next decade, the *chaebol* discarded its core market and became one of the world's leading industrial- and construction-equipment manufacturers, a change punctuated by its acquisition of the US manufacturer Bobcat, in 2007. Yongmaan Park, the chairman of Doosan Infracore and the force behind the group's globalization, discusses the transformation and his ideas on talent integration at home and abroad.

The *Quarterly*: *What was your approach toward integrating talent?*

Yongmaan Park: After we acquired Doosan Heavy and Doosan Infracore, we tried to visualize the future. When we looked three or four years ahead, we saw an organization in which 70 to 80 percent of our people would have been with us for less than five years. How would we maintain our competitive strengths? We needed to create an organization that would deliver our philosophy and values to these new kids. How would we do that?

We started by interviewing more than 300 people who had experience working with us, who had experience working with my late father. We tried to pull out the management philosophies that gave us the strength to survive the crisis and had supported us for the last 100 years. These centered on integrity and *inhwa*, which can be translated as harmonious relations or harmonious teamwork. In the Korean workplace, *inhwa* has typically meant smooth relationships among peers, as well as between leaders and those who report to them. At Doosan, we focus on how to create a harmonious work environment. We acknowledge differences,

adhere to fair rules, and build a cooperative, collaborative, and positive workplace. During this effort, we also tried to visualize what philosophy would help us become a strong, truly global company.

In the end, we decided that three areas of focus would carry our philosophy and values into the daily life of our corporate citizens: human resources, strategic planning, and evaluation and control. While other Asian companies were trying to infuse their values into new acquisitions through people, we wanted to infuse our values through management processes. Those are clearly two different ways of doing things.

The *Quarterly*: *Let's focus on the Bobcat acquisition. What was the atmosphere as you were approaching that deal?*

Yongmaan Park: We were excited because we had been arguing that we needed to globalize. We understood the necessity, but we weren't sure how to proceed; the only global experience we had was in exporting. But at the same time, there was a lot of fear. We had never managed a global company before. Could we do it?

The full interview is available on mckinseyquarterly.com.

'At Doosan, we focus on how to create a harmonious work environment'

Yongmaan Park
Chairman
Doosan Infracore

For the people at Bobcat, we were a big question mark: who the hell are these guys? All of the other contenders were well-known companies in the construction industry. Most of the Bobcat managers had never had a chance to come to Korea, hadn't had a chance to meet Korean people, let alone to hear about a company named Doosan. One of the first questions they asked me was, what would we do with the Bobcat brand? I told them that we're paying a lot of money to buy this company. Its value is supported by many things, but clearly the brand is an important factor. My initial reaction was, why should I get rid of it? But I added that the decision on the brand does not belong to me; it has to come from our customers.

The *Quarterly*: *Will you integrate Bobcat differently from the way you integrated your domestic acquisitions?*

Yongmaan Park: When we acquired Doosan Heavy, the total number of employees was 7,000. I sent about a dozen people into that operation, including very junior people. When we acquired Doosan Infracore, I did the same thing. With Bobcat, again the same. I don't need to send in an army of people and create a shadow management. That just shows that you have no confidence in the local people or that you are afraid they do not share the same values. As I've said, we instill those values through processes.

When we acquired Bobcat, we created an introductory package containing our credo, our brochure, and our company badge, and we distributed it to every single employee. One of my guys suggested we also include a nice English book about Korea. He said we need to show them what our country is about so they can understand who we are. I said, what for? These guys at Bobcat don't need to learn about Korea from us, but they do need to learn how we manage the company, what our competitive strengths are. That's the thing they have to learn from us, not about Korea.

We want to become a global company that happens to be from Korea. Nestlé is a good example. Most people, even the business community, don't see the color and taste of Switzerland in Nestlé. It's simply a multinational company that happened to originate in Switzerland. I want to build Doosan to be such a global company. That's our aspiration, and it tells us not to oversell Korea.

Dominic Barton is a director in McKinsey's Shanghai office, and **Clay Deutsch** is a director in the Boston office.

The Quarterly *Surveys*

Selected results from surveys of the *Quarterly*'s panel of global executives

Mobilizing employees for change

Achieving a true step change in performance is rare. Indeed, only three executives in ten say their organization's transformation efforts succeed in doing so. These companies are much likelier than less successful ones to clearly define goals for change that are truly transformational, and to have a CEO who is highly involved and visible in the effort.

They also use a much wider variety of tactics to engage the whole organization—an average of 5.1 tactics compared with 1.6 at companies where respondents consider the transformation not at all successful. Engaging the organization through ongoing communication and involvement (such as celebrating successes) edges out holding people accountable for results as the tactic used most frequently by the most successful companies. What's interesting is that this tactic drops to third place among all respondents and to fifth place among those who say the transformation was not at all successful. Even some of the most successful companies, however, can do more to ensure that front-line workers feel ownership of the change—more than a quarter of their executives say they would spend more time engaging these employees if they had to undertake the transformation again.

From "Creating organizational transformations: McKinsey Global Survey Results," August 2008, which includes the responses of 3,199 executives from around the world.

% of respondents[1]

How visible was the CEO's or business unit leader's involvement in the transformation?

	Success of transformation			
	Not successful at all, n = 144	Somewhat successful, n = 1,519	Very successful, n = 835	Extremely successful, n = 165
Not at all visible	23	6	3	1
Not very visible	29	22	10	13
Fairly visible	32	37	31	25
Very visible	16	35	56	61

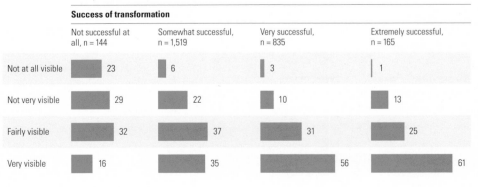

[1]Excludes respondents who answered "don't know"; data are weighted by GDPs of constituent countries to adjust for differences in response rates.

The full results of these surveys are available on mckinseyquarterly.com/surveys.

Complexity and risk in **global supply chains**

Supply chain risk is rising sharply. More than three-quarters of executives say the degree of supply chain risk their companies face has increased over the past five years, up from less than two-thirds who said the same two years ago. They point to the greater complexity of products and services, higher energy prices, and increasing financial volatility as top factors influencing their supply chain strategies. Despite the importance respondents place on these trends, however, relatively few say that their companies are acting on them. For example, only 35 and 16 percent of the executives say that their companies have acted in response to the increasing complexity of products and services and to rising energy prices, respectively. When companies do act on trends, the most common responses are increasing the efficiency of supply chain processes, actively managing risks along the supply chain, and sourcing more inputs from low-cost countries.

When setting strategic goals for supply chains, companies focus first on reducing costs and then on improving customer service and getting new products or services to market faster. But fewer than half of the executives indicate that their companies completely or almost completely meet any strategic supply chain goal.

From "Managing global supply chains: McKinsey Global Survey Results," August 2008, which includes the responses of 273 executives from around the world.

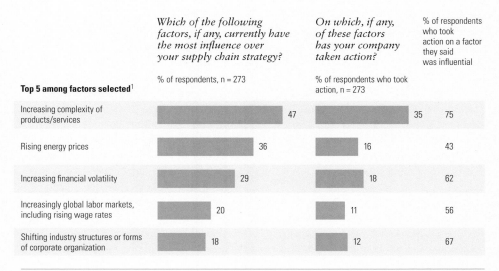

Top 5 among factors selected[1]	Which of the following factors, if any, currently have the most influence over your supply chain strategy? % of respondents, n = 273	On which, if any, of these factors has your company taken action? % of respondents who took action, n = 273	% of respondents who took action on a factor they said was influential
Increasing complexity of products/services	47	35	75
Rising energy prices	36	16	43
Increasing financial volatility	29	18	62
Increasingly global labor markets, including rising wage rates	20	11	56
Shifting industry structures or forms of corporate organization	18	12	67

[1]Respondents could select up to 3 answers.

A fresh wind for offshoring
infrastructure management

Vivek Pandit and Rajesh Srinivasaraghavan

Businesses have begun tapping offshore companies to monitor, maintain, and fix their IT infrastructures. Revenues from remote infrastructure management, as these services are called, have grown by 80 percent a year since 2005 and are expected to reach $6 billion to $7 billion this year. But our research shows that the possibilities for managing servers and other IT hardware from afar are largely untapped. Changes in the business environment could let loose a sudden rush to adopt this approach.

While customers have enthusiastically offshored application development and business processes, remote infrastructure management has languished by comparison. Our estimates suggest that at the end of 2007, such revenues accounted for less than 7 percent of an addressable market of $96 billion to $104 billion, despite a steady increase in recent years. But within half a decade, those revenues could grow fourfold, reaching $26 billion to $28 billion annually.

The benefits of remote infrastructure management can be considerable—Fortune 50 companies, with budgets of $2 billion, can save as much as $500 million of their IT infrastructure budgets, mostly from labor savings. Yet there are also risks. Disruptions in core IT systems during the transition or ongoing operations have real financial and security costs, including possible data loss and the interruption of operations. Other concerns include regulatory problems, such as the possibility of giving third parties inadvertent access to confidential medical records, and of financial fraud or intellectual-property (IP) theft when vendors gain full access to corporate systems.

Nonetheless, a change in customer attitudes confirms the growth potential. We surveyed 141 CIOs at multinational corporations in 2007, and 34 percent of them say they expect to offshore some infrastructure services over the next three years—a sharp increase from 19 percent in a similar survey a year earlier. The responses suggest that the growth will encompass a broad swath of remote-management opportunities, including storage, help-desk, server, and network services (Exhibit 1).

A change in the economics lies behind the expected growth. As hardware costs

EXHIBIT I

A likely increase

% of respondents (n = 141)[1]

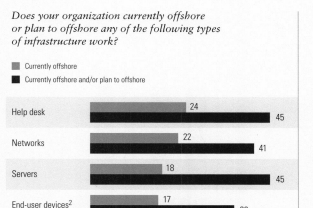

*Does your organization currently offshore
or plan to offshore any of the following types
of infrastructure work?*

■ Currently offshore
■ Currently offshore and/or plan to offshore

Help desk	24	45
Networks	22	41
Servers	18	45
End-user devices[2]	17	36
Mainframes	15	33
Storage	13	41

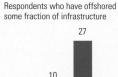

Respondents who have offshored
some fraction of infrastructure

27
10
2006   2007

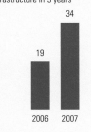

Respondents who plan to offshore
infrastructure in 3 years

34
19
2006   2007

[1] Excludes those who do not plan to offshore.
[2] For example, desktops, laptops, PDAs.

Source: 2006 and 2007 McKinsey surveys of CIOs; McKinsey analysis

fall, labor has become the most addressable cost in infrastructure. We estimate that costs for nonlabor components—hardware, software, maintenance (for instance, software updates and hardware replacement), and facilities—declined by almost 44 percent between 2000 and 2008 as competitive pressures, innovation, and tougher negotiations with vendors brought prices down. Between 2008 and 2010, nonlabor costs are expected to fall by 54 percent, thanks to innovations such as virtualization, which essentially allows several hardware components to act as a single component or, conversely, a single component to act as several separate ones. Total costs will fall by nearly half from 2000 to 2010, while labor's share (largely infrastructure management) will more than double, to 62 percent, from 30 percent (Exhibit 2).

Changes in the deployment of infrastructure have also made remote management more attractive for a growing list of companies. Many have simplified their IT architecture; for example, the marketing division of a global pharmaceutical company consolidated 95 servers, each running a different version of an operating system, into just 7, with standard configurations. Standardization makes repetitive tasks such as updating virus definitions easier to automate, and improved documentation allows complex tasks to be broken up into a series of simpler steps that less-skilled workers can undertake. As a result, it is easier

EXHIBIT 2

Labor: The most addressable cost

% of respondents (n = 141)

Hardware prices have rapidly declined . . .

Average selling price, $

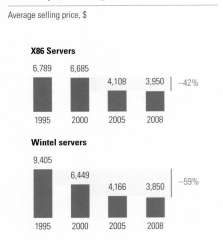

. . . making labor and software key cost savings levers.

Estimated total cost of ownership for a server, $ a year

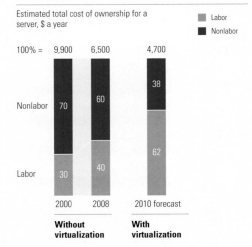

Source: Forrester 2005; IDC; Meta 2004; McKinsey analysis

to manage complex tasks from remote locations.

At the same time, customers have grown more sophisticated: they can judiciously outsource selected parts of infrastructure management while retaining control over critical ones. Some companies, for example, have outsourced only network monitoring; others, the total management and ownership of existing data centers. Many more infrastructure contracts are being signed, and individual deals tend to be smaller and to cover shorter periods; between 2002 and 2007, the average contract's value dropped by more than 70 percent, the average duration by more than 20 percent. Both trends give companies greater flexibility when contracting with different vendors.

The greater speed and security of data communication has made interactions between companies and their outsourcers easier and more stable and thus increased their level of comfort with outsourcing. A critical mass of sophisticated vendors has emerged as well. In 2000, for example, 84 percent of the largest infrastructure-management outsourcing contracts went to the top six vendors, but by 2007 they were capturing just 54 percent. This shift gives customers greater confidence in the outsourcers' ability to provide and retain qualified workers to staff a growing number of projects.

Although remote infrastructure management has become more attractive, challenges remain. Disruptions brought on by the transition still carry real costs. Planning and implementation can take four months to a year and generally involve changes in a company's IT and communications architectures, as well as investments in software for remote troubleshooting and enhanced security within networks. Additionally, roles in a company's IT organization usually change.

To overcome these obstacles, a company considering the benefits of remote infrastructure management should collaborate with vendors early in its deliberations. The topics for discussion include which company holds responsibility for each aspect of the project, the planning of the transition, and performance metrics. A company taking this route should also design its management structure from a clean slate rather than tweak current systems to fit a vendor's model.

Vivek Pandit is a principal and **Rajesh Srinivasaraghavan** is a consultant in McKinsey's Mumbai office.

Illustrations by Serge Bloch/Marlena Agency.

We welcome your comments on these articles.
Please send them to quarterly_comments@mckinsey.com.

The crisis:

A new era in management

Artwork by Daniel Hertzberg

Leading through uncertainty

The range of possible futures confronting business is great. Companies that nurture flexibility, awareness, and resiliency are more likely to survive the crisis, and even to prosper.

Lowell Bryan and Diana Farrell

The future of capitalism is here, and it's not what any of us expected. With breathtaking speed, in the autumn of 2008 the credit markets ceased functioning normally, governments around the world began nationalizing financial systems and considering bailouts of other troubled industries, and major independent US investment banks disappeared or became bank holding companies. Meanwhile, currency values, as well as oil and other commodity prices, lurched wildly, while housing prices in Spain, the United Kingdom, the United States, and elsewhere continued to slide.

As consumers batten down the hatches and the global economy slows, senior executives confront a more profoundly uncertain business environment than most of them have ever faced. Uncertainty surrounds not only the downturn's depth and duration—though these are decidedly big unknowns—but also the very future of a global economic order until recently characterized by free-flowing capital and trade and by ever-deepening economic ties. A few months ago, the only challenges to this global system seemed to be external ones like climate change, terrorism, and war. Now, every day brings news that makes all of us wonder if the system itself will survive.

Lowell Bryan is a director in McKinsey's New York office, and **Diana Farrell** is director of the McKinsey Global Institute.

The task of business leaders must be to overcome the paralysis that dooms any organization and to begin shaping the future. One starting

point is to take stock of what they do know about their industries and the surrounding economic environment; such an understanding will probably suggest needed changes in strategy. Even then, enormous uncertainty will remain, particularly about how governments will behave and how the global real economy and financial system will interact. All these factors, taken together, will determine whether we face just a few declining quarters, a severe global recession, or something in between.

Uncertainty of this magnitude will leave some leaders lost in the fog. To avoid impulsive, uncoordinated, and ultimately ineffective responses, companies must evaluate an unusually broad set of macroeconomic outcomes and strategic responses and then act to make themselves more flexible, aware, and resilient.

Strengthening these organizational muscles will allow companies not only to survive but also to seize the extraordinary opportunities that arise during periods of vast uncertainty. It was during the recessionary 1870s that John Rockefeller and Andrew Carnegie began grabbing dominant positions in the emerging oil and steel industries by taking advantage of new refining and steel production technologies and of the weakness of competitors. A century later, also in a difficult economy, Warren Buffett converted a struggling textile company called Berkshire Hathaway into a source of funds for far-flung investments.

What we know

The financial electricity that drives our global economy is not working well. Turning it back on isn't just a matter of flicking a switch, as central banks and governments have tried to do by providing liquidity, guaranteeing debt, and injecting capital into banks. We must repair the grid itself significantly, and this will require coordinated global action.

By the grid, we mean the global capital market, which evolved over a 35-year period following the breakdown of the Bretton Woods accord, in the 1970s. No one designed the global capital market, but it has been a boon to humanity, stimulating globalization and growth by enabling the free international flow of capital and trade. The financial crisis of 2008 severely damaged this useful system. Through greed, neglect, or ignorance, the participants abused it until they broke some of its basic mechanisms.

The implications are far reaching. Most obviously, congestion in the global capital market is exacerbating the US domestic credit crisis. That crisis has spread globally, hitting Europe especially hard. Banks until recently have been scrambling for deposits to replace sources of funding such as direct-issue commercial paper, medium-term notes, and asset-backed paper. The search for deposits is required to finance existing loans, and borrowers will need significantly more of them because all but the strongest have, like the banks, lost access to the securities markets. The US government, in particular, has aggressively tried to address this problem through huge liquidity programs, such as the purchase of mortgage- and other asset-backed securities. But it remains to be seen how effective those efforts will be in mitigating the credit crunch.

The global capital market crisis worsens this credit crunch by reversing the dynamic of cross-border investment and trade flows. A dollar of capital must finance every dollar of trade, so the global capital market has stimulated the international exchange of goods and services. It has facilitated cross-border investments—in intellectual property, talent, brands, and networks—that help economies and companies grow and profit, and it has enabled the companies that make such investments to repatriate their profits. In short, global integration and growth will revive only if the global capital market does. Yet it has sustained a body blow that will have repercussions for years, even if international leaders make the necessary long-term adjustments.

The changing role of government

Since September 2008, governments have assumed a dramatically expanded role in financial markets. Policy makers have gone to great lengths to stabilize them, to support individual companies whose failure might pose systemic risks, and to prevent a deep economic downturn. We can expect higher tax rates to pay for these moves, as well as for the reregulation of finance and many other sectors. In short, governments will have their hand in industry to an extent few imagined possible only recently.

That's not all. Protectionism and nationalism will probably feature more prominently in policy debates. We may see not only old-style populist anger against business, high executive compensation, and layoffs but also the emergence of authoritarian populist movements. Already-dilatory trade discussions will encounter renewed resistance. Although greater global coordination is sorely needed, national political pressures will make it hard to achieve. All this will constrain some business activities but also opens the door to new ventures that depend upon collaboration between the public and private sectors.

Deleveraging

The cheap credit of the past few years most likely won't return for a long time. For many households, this will mean reducing consumption and postponing retirement; for financial institutions—increasingly, bank holding companies—much higher capital requirements, less freedom to operate and innovate, and probably lower profitability; for governments, even more limited resources for health care, education, pensions, infrastructure, the environment, and security; and for corporations, a different role for capital. More broadly, for many companies the high returns and rapid growth of recent years rested on

cheap credit, so deleveraging means that expectations of baseline profitability and economic growth, as well as shareholder returns, must all be seriously recalibrated.

New business models and industry restructuring

Companies engaging with the capital markets will encounter funders who are less tolerant of risk, a reduced ability to hedge it, and greater volatility. Hardest hit will be business models premised on high leverage, consumer credit, large customer-financing operations, or high levels of working capital. Businesses with long or inflexible production cycles or very long-term investment requirements will find it especially difficult to manage their funding. Some won't make it, so industries will restructure. Corporate leaders already recognize this: in a *McKinsey Quarterly* executive survey launched the day after the US presidential election, 54 percent of the respondents expected their industries to consolidate.

These are all truths we know. They require a significant shift in thinking about government as a stakeholder, the value talent creates when it is harder to leverage, how to conserve capital, and strategies for sound risk taking—among other things.

What we don't know

Yet there is much that we don't know, and won't for some time: how well will governments work together to develop effective regulatory, trade, fiscal, and monetary policies; what will these responses mean for the long-term health of the global capital market; how will its health or weakness influence the pace and extent of change in areas such as the economic role of government, financial leverage, and business models; and what will all this imply for globalization and economic growth?

Although these questions won't be answered in the short or even the medium term, decisions made in the immediate future are critical, for they will influence how well organizations manage themselves now and compete over the longer haul. The winners will be companies that make thoughtful choices—despite the complexity, confusion, and uncertainty—by assessing alternative scenarios honestly, considering their implications, and preparing accordingly.

In particular, organizations must think expansively about the possibilities. Even in more normal times, the range of outcomes most companies consider is too narrow. The assumptions used for budgeting and business planning are often modest variations on baseline projections whose major assumptions often are not presented explicitly. Many such budgets and plans are soon overtaken by events. In normal times, that matters little because companies continually adapt to the environment, and budgets usually build in conservative assumptions so managers can beat their numbers.

EXHIBIT

Hard, harder, hardest times

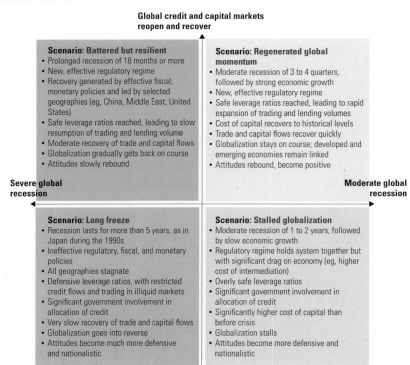

Global credit and capital markets
reopen and recover

Scenario: Battered but resilient
- Prolonged recession of 18 months or more
- New, effective regulatory regime
- Recovery generated by effective fiscal, monetary policies and led by selected geographies (eg, China, Middle East, United States)
- Safe leverage ratios reached, leading to slow resumption of trading and lending volume
- Moderate recovery of trade and capital flows
- Globalization gradually gets back on course
- Attitudes slowly rebound

Scenario: Regenerated global momentum
- Moderate recession of 3 to 4 quarters, followed by strong economic growth
- New, effective regulatory regime
- Safe leverage ratios reached, leading to rapid expansion of trading and lending volumes
- Cost of capital recovers to historical levels
- Trade and capital flows recover quickly
- Globalization stays on course; developed and emerging economies remain linked
- Attitudes rebound, become positive

Severe global recession ← → Moderate global recession

Scenario: Long freeze
- Recession lasts for more than 5 years, as in Japan during the 1990s
- Ineffective regulatory, fiscal, and monetary policies
- All geographies stagnate
- Defensive leverage ratios, with restricted credit flows and trading in illiquid markets
- Significant government involvement in allocation of credit
- Very slow recovery of trade and capital flows
- Globalization goes into reverse
- Attitudes become much more defensive and nationalistic

Scenario: Stalled globalization
- Moderate recession of 1 to 2 years, followed by slow economic growth
- Regulatory regime holds system together but with significant drag on economy (eg, higher cost of intermediation)
- Overly safe leverage ratios
- Significant government involvement in allocation of credit
- Significantly higher cost of capital than before crisis
- Globalization stalls
- Attitudes become more defensive and nationalistic

Global credit and capital markets
close down and remain volatile

But these are not normal times: the range of potential outcomes—the uncertainty surrounding the global credit crisis and the global recession—is so large that many companies may not survive. We can capture this wide range of outcomes in four scenarios (exhibit).

To see them in perspective, consider some results of the McKinsey Global Institute's research (see sidebar, "The credit crunch and the real economy"). This research, focusing on the United States, the center of the storm, suggests that if capital markets rebound quickly, GDP would be 2.9 percentage points lower than it would have been if trend growth had continued over the next two years. If financial markets take longer to recover, as the middle two scenarios envision, US GDP growth could fall 4.7 to 6.7 percentage points from trend over the same period. At the "long freeze" end of the spectrum, Japan's "lost decade" shaved 18 percentage points from GDP compared with its previous growth trend.

Regenerated global momentum

In the most optimistic scenario, government action revives the global credit system—the massive stimulus packages and aggressive monetary policies already adopted keep the global recession from lasting very long or being very deep. Globalization stays on course: trade and capital flows resume quickly, and the developed and emerging economies continue to integrate as confidence rebounds quickly.

Battered but resilient

In the second scenario, government-wrought improvements in the global credit and capital market are more than offset—for 18 months or more—by the impact of the global recession, which leads to further credit losses and to distrust of cross-border counterparties. Although the recession could be longer and deeper than any in the past 70 years, government action works, and the global capital and credit markets gradually recover. Global confidence, though shaken, does rebound, and trade and capital flows revive moderately. Globalization slowly gets back on course.

Stalled globalization

In the third scenario, the global recession is significant, but its intensity varies greatly from nation to nation—in particular, China and the United States prove surprisingly resilient. The integration of the world's economies, however, stalls as continuing fear of counterparties makes the global capital market less integrated. Trade flows and capital flows decline and then stagnate. The regulatory regime holds the system together, but various governments overregulate lending and risk, so the world's banking system becomes "oversafe." Credit remains expensive and hard to get. As attitudes become more defensive and nationalistic, growth is relatively slow.

The long freeze

Under the final scenario, the global recession lasts more than five years (as Japan's did in the 1990s) because of ineffective regulatory, fiscal, and monetary policy. Economies everywhere stagnate; overregulation and fear keep the global credit and capital markets closed. Trade and capital flows continue to decline for years as globalization goes into reverse, and the psychology of nations becomes much more defensive and nationalistic.

Leading through uncertainty

These descriptions are intentionally stylized to enliven them; many permutations are possible. Scenarios for any company and industry should of course be tailored to individual circumstances. What we hope to illustrate is the importance for strategists of considering previously unthinkable outcomes, such as the rollback of globalization. Unappealing as three of the four scenarios may be, any company that sets its strategy without taking all of them into account is flying blind.

So executives need a way of operating that's suited to the most uncertain business environment since the 1930s. They need greater

The credit crunch and the real economy

Diana Farrell and
Susan Lund

Something extraordinary happened from mid-2007 to mid-2008: net new borrowing by US households and companies plunged 65 percent ($1.4 trillion). This drop abruptly reversed recent trends. During the previous eight years, borrowing had grown by 2.4 percent a year, much faster than it did from 1970 to 2000, when the rate was 0.9 percent.

Credit growth has been correlated with faster GDP growth—consumer borrowing fuels sales of homes, autos, consumer electronics, and more; businesses issue debt to finance new plants and construction. Deleveraging will therefore have a significant effect on the real economy. To understand that impact, we assessed how much further borrowing by households and companies could decline over the next two years in each of the five channels they use to obtain credit and then modeled the resulting reduction in US GDP growth.

1. Loans from banks: US banks are still writing off credit losses and facing rising defaults on many types of loans. McKinsey analysis suggests that total credit losses on US loans could reach $1.4 trillion to $2.2 trillion, eroding bank equity.[1] Although banks have raised new capital from the government and private investors, the credit crunch will continue for some time. After taking into account recapitalization, the reduction in bank leverage ratios, and taxes, we calculate that bank lending to US households and companies could decline by $1.9 trillion to $3.5 trillion from trend over the next two years.[2]

2. Lending by nonbank intermediaries: Companies also borrow from pension funds, insurance companies, and the government. This $1.7 trillion source of credit has already been drying up. We assume that this trend will continue over the coming two years as these intermediaries regroup after suffering large portfolio losses.

3. Debt owned or securitized by government-sponsored enterprises, such as Fannie Mae and Freddie Mac: These

Diana Farrell
is director of
the McKinsey Global
Institute, where
Susan Lund is a
consultant.

giant entities account for nearly 40 percent of credit to US households ($5.1 trillion in the second quarter of 2008). This is the only channel that has increased its lending throughout the crisis, offsetting some of the private-sector credit reduction. We assume that this countercyclical lending activity will continue, offsetting part of the reduction in credit through other channels.

4. Corporate bond and commercial-paper markets: Borrowing through debt capital markets in the form of bonds or commercial paper is a major source of funding to companies, second only to banks. Although issuance by investment-grade nonfinancial companies declined only modestly, high-yield bonds have declined much more sharply. In our model, issuance continues to decline for the next several quarters and revives in 2009 and 2010 in different recession scenarios.

5. Securitization markets: Borrowing through private lenders that securitize mortgages, consumer debt, and commercial loans has fallen sharply during the crisis. In our most severe deleveraging scenario, we assume that only the plain-vanilla forms of securitization revive, while some of the more exotic structured products do not.

Adding up the reduction of credit through each of the five channels, we estimate that US household and corporate borrowing could decline by an additional $1.6 trillion to $3.7 trillion over the next two years, depending on the size of credit losses and the speed of the capital markets' recovery. US economic growth is likely to slow significantly as a result (exhibit).

A $1.6 trillion drop implies that US real GDP would be 2.9 percentage points lower than trend growth over the next two years—less than it fell during the recession following the US savings and loan crisis of the 1980s. In a $2.6 trillion drop, credit losses would spread from mortgages to credit cards, car loans, and other forms of consumer debt, and credit markets would remain tight through the third quarter of 2009. The resulting cumulative decline in GDP from trend would be 4.7 percentage points through mid-2010. That would be the worst US recession since

1981 and worse than the financial crises in other developed countries, such as Finland, Sweden, and the United Kingdom. Finally, a $3.7 trillion drop would reflect much larger credit losses for banks and tight credit markets through the middle of 2010 as a result of continuing declines in corporate profits and home prices. The cumulative GDP decline through mid-2010 would be 6.7 percentage points compared with trend.

Each of these scenarios depends on many assumptions and comes with caveats, which offer cause for either hope or worry. The actual GDP loss might be lower, for example, if the government's aggressive policy responses work. Conversely, the results could be worse if an unexpectedly large decline in household wealth causes a steeper decline in consumer spending, if US business confidence erodes more rapidly and severely than in previous recessions, if the securities market remains inaccessible to banks and other corporate borrowers for an extended time,

if the global capital market proves hard to repair, or if economic pain triggers a protectionist backlash that derails globalization.

The worst of these possibilities would occur only if policy makers and business leaders made serious mistakes of the sort that produced Japan's "lost decade" (which shaved 18 percentage points off GDP growth) and the Great Depression (with its cumulative GDP loss of nearly 40 percentage points compared with trend). Job one for government and business leaders today is to avoid repeating those mistakes.

[1] Work by the International Monetary Fund and others suggests that one-third of the losses on US loans are borne by US banks, the remainder by European and other foreign banks, as well as pension funds, hedge funds, and other investors in the United States and abroad.

[2] Total bank credit to households and companies, as of the second quarter of 2008, was $10.8 trillion. We assume that trend growth is in line with GDP growth, which is 2.5 percent in real terms.

EXHIBIT

An uncertain future: Three scenarios for deleveraging

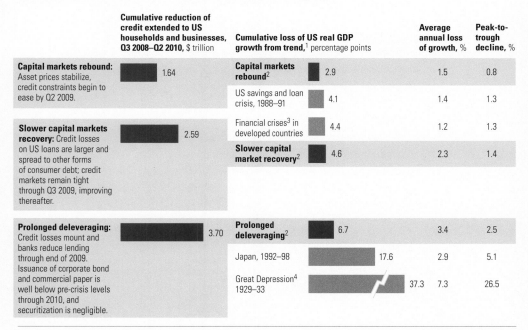

	Cumulative reduction of credit extended to US households and businesses, Q3 2008–Q2 2010, $ trillion	Cumulative loss of US real GDP growth from trend,[1] percentage points		Average annual loss of growth, %	Peak-to-trough decline, %
Capital markets rebound: Asset prices stabilize, credit constraints begin to ease by Q2 2009.	1.64	Capital markets rebound[2]	2.9	1.5	0.8
		US savings and loan crisis, 1988–91	4.1	1.4	1.3
Slower capital markets recovery: Credit losses on US loans are larger and spread to other forms of consumer debt; credit markets remain tight through Q3 2009, improving thereafter.	2.59	Financial crises[3] in developed countries	4.4	1.2	1.3
		Slower capital market recovery[2]	4.6	2.3	1.4
Prolonged deleveraging: Credit losses mount and banks reduce lending through end of 2009. Issuance of corporate bond and commercial paper is well below pre-crisis levels through 2010, and securitization is negligible.	3.70	Prolonged deleveraging[2]	6.7	3.4	2.5
		Japan, 1992–98	17.6	2.9	5.1
		Great Depression[4] 1929–33	37.3	7.3	26.5

[1] Impact of credit reduction on GDP growth estimated using historical relationship between credit and GDP growth; based on 2008 research by Jan Hatzius.
[2] Peak-to-trough declines are estimated by replicating the typical growth path of external forecasts.
[3] Median cumulative loss of GDP from crises in Australia, Austria, Belgium, Canada, Denmark, Finland, France, Germany, Italy, Japan, Netherlands, Norway, Spain, Sweden, Switzerland, United Kingdom, and United States (savings and loan crisis).
[4] Estimated using annual data. Growth-rate trend was estimated using the Hodrick-Prescott filter and averaged over 5 years prior to crisis.

Source: Global Insight; International Monetary Fund (IMF); McKinsey Global Institute analysis

flexibility to create strategic and tactical options they can use defensively and offensively as conditions change. They need a sharper awareness of their own and their competitors' positions. And they need to make their organizations more resilient.

Most companies acted immediately in the autumn of 2008 when credit markets locked up: they cut discretionary spending, slowed investment, managed cash flows aggressively, laid off employees, shored up financing sources, and built capital by cutting dividends, raising equity, and so forth. While prudent, these actions probably won't produce the short-term earnings that analysts expect, at least for most companies. In fact, it's time they abandoned the idea that they can reliably deliver predictable earnings. Quarterly performance is no longer the objective, which must now be to ensure the long-term survival and health of the enterprise.

More flexible

Companies must now take a more flexible approach to planning: each of them should develop several coherent, multipronged strategic-action plans, not just one. Every plan should embrace all of the functions, business units, and geographies of a company and show how it can make the most of a specific economic environment.

These plans can't be academic exercises; executives must be ready to pursue any of them—quickly—as the future unfolds. In fact, the broad range of plausible outcomes in today's business environment calls for a "just in time" approach to strategy setting, risk taking, and resource allocation by senior executives. A company's 10 to 20 top managers, for example, might have weekly or even daily "all hands on deck" meetings to exchange information and make fast operational decisions.

Greater flexibility also means developing as many options as possible that can be exercised either when trigger events occur or the future becomes more certain. Often, options will be offensive moves. Which acquisitions could be attractive on what terms, for instance, and how much capital and management capacity would be required? What new products best fit different scenarios? If one or more major competitors should falter, how will the company react? In which markets can it gain share?

As companies prepare for such opportunities, they should also create options to maintain good health under difficult circumstances. If capital market breakdowns make global sourcing too risky, for example, companies that restructure their supply chains quickly will be in much better shape. If changes in the global economy could make a certain kind of business unit obsolete, it's critical to finish all the preparatory work needed to sell it before every company with that kind of unit reaches the same conclusion.

A crisis tends to surface options—such as how to slash structural costs while minimizing damage to long-term competitiveness—that organizations ordinarily wouldn't consider. Unless executives evaluate their options early on, they could later find themselves moving with too little information or preparation and therefore make faulty decisions, delay action, or forgo options altogether.

More aware

As problems with credit destroy and remake business models and market volatility whipsaws valuations, companies desperately need to understand how their revenues, costs, profits, cash flows, risks, and balance sheets will fare under different scenarios. With that information, executives can plan for the worst even as they hope for the best. If the recession lasted more than five years, for example, could the company survive? Is it prepared for the bankruptcy of major customers? Could it halve capital spending quickly? The answers should help companies to be better prepared and to recognize, as early as possible, which scenario is developing. That is critical knowledge in a crisis, when lead times disappear quickly and companies can seize the initiative only if they act before the entire world understands the probable outcome.

Better business intelligence promotes faster, more effective decision making as well. Companies can often gain insights into the potential moves of competitors by weighing news reports about their activities, stock analyst reports, and private information gathered by talking to customers and suppliers. Such intelligence is always important; in a crisis it can make the difference between missing opportunities to buy distressed assets and leaping in to snare them.

To get this kind of business intelligence, companies need a network, typically led by someone with strong support from the top. This executive's mandate should include creating "eyes and ears" across businesses and geographies in particular areas of focus (such as the competition's response to the crisis), as well as gathering and exchanging information. A network is critical because information is most useful if it moves not just vertically, up and down the organization, but also horizontally. Salespeople in a network, for example, should exchange knowledge about what's working in economically distressed regions so that employees can help each other.

Assembling bits of information, facts, and anecdotes helps companies to make sense of what's happening in an industry. Say, for example, that a supplier says it has no difficulties with funding, though firsthand knowledge from other sources indicates that the company is struggling to meet its payroll. Such warnings can allow executives to get a full picture much more quickly than they could by sitting in their offices and interacting only with direct subordinates.

More resilient

A crisis is a chance to break ingrained structures and behaviors that sap the productivity and effectiveness of many organizations. Such moves aren't a short-term crisis response—they often take a year or more to pay dividends—but are valuable in any scenario and could help a company survive if hard times persist. Although employees may dislike this approach, most will understand why management aims to make the organization more effective.

This may, for example, be the time to destroy the vertical organizational structures, retrofitted with ad hoc and matrix overlays, that encumber companies large and small. Such structures can burden professionals with several competing bosses. Internecine battles and unclear decisions are common. Turf wars between product, sales, and geographic managers kill promising projects. Searches for information aren't productive, and countless hours are wasted on pointless e-mails, telephone calls, and meetings.

Experience shows that streamlining an organization to define roles and the way those who hold them collaborate can greatly improve its effectiveness and decision making. When jobs must be eliminated, the cuts mostly reduce unproductive complexity rather than valuable work. As Matthew Guthridge, John R. McPherson, and William J. Wolf point out in "Smart cost cutting in the downturn: Upgrading talent" (in this issue), Cisco took that approach in shedding 8,500 jobs in 2001. When the company redesigned roles and responsibilities to improve cooperation among functions and reduce duplication of effort, talented employees were more satisfied in a more collaborative workplace.

The authors wish to thank David Atkins, Kevin Buehler, Jared Chung, Ezra Greenberg, Jeff Gu, Bill Hoffman, Susan Lund, Christopher Mazingo, Kazuhiro Ninomiya, Hamid Samandari, and Elizabeth Stephenson for their contributions to this article and the research underlying it.

In fact, many functional areas offer big opportunities: greater effectiveness, lower fixed costs, freed-up capital, and reduced risk. This could be the moment to redefine and reprioritize the use of IT to increase its impact and cut its cost. Other companies could seize the moment to control inventory; to reexamine their cash flow management, including payments and receivables; or to change the mix of marketing vehicles and sales models in response to the rising cost of traditional media and the growing effectiveness of new ones.

We welcome your comments on this article. Please send them to quarterly_comments@ mckinsey.com.

As customer preferences change, competitors falter, opportunities to gain distressed assets emerge, and governments shift from crisis control to economic stimulus, the next year or two will probably produce new laggards, leaders, and industry dynamics. The future will belong to companies whose senior executives remain calm, carefully assess their options, and nurture the flexibility, awareness, and resiliency needed to deal with whatever the world throws at them.

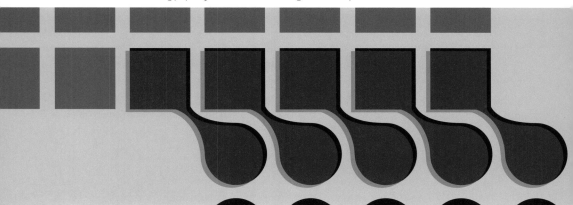

Strategy in a 'structural break'

During hard times, a structural break in the economy is an opportunity in disguise. To survive—and, eventually, to flourish—companies must learn to exploit it.

Richard P. Rumelt

There is nothing like a crisis to clarify the mind. In suddenly volatile and different times, you must have a strategy. I don't mean most of the things people call strategy—mission statements, audacious goals, three-to five-year budget plans. I mean a real strategy.

For many managers, the word has become a verbal tic. Business lingo has transformed marketing into marketing strategy, data processing into IT strategy, acquisitions into growth strategy. Cut prices and you have a low-price strategy. Equating strategy with success, audacity, or ambition creates still more confusion. A lot of people label anything that bears the CEO's signature as strategic—a definition based on the decider's pay grade, not the decision.

By strategy, I mean a cohesive response to a challenge. A real strategy is neither a document nor a forecast but rather an overall approach based on a diagnosis of a challenge. The most important element of a strategy is a coherent viewpoint about the forces at work, not a plan.

What's happening?

The past year's events have been surprising but not novel. Historically, land bubbles, easy credit, and high leverage often make a dangerous mixture. Real-estate debt triggered the first US depression, in 1819. A land mortgage boom was directly behind the 1873–77 crisis: innova-

Richard Rumelt is the Harry and Elsa Kunin professor of business and society at the Anderson School of Management, University of California at Los Angeles.

tive forms of mortgage lending in Europe and the United States generated an unsustainable boom in land prices, and a four-year global depression followed their collapse and the accompanying credit crunch. Another credit crunch, this one triggered by the failure of traded railroad notes, led to the Long Depression of 1893–97. Japan's 1995–2004 "lost decade" followed a period of high leverage and wildly inflated land values brought to an end by a financial crash.

Leverage lies at the heart of such stories. Archimedes said, "Give me a lever long enough and a fulcrum strong enough, and I will move the world." He didn't add that it would take a lever many light years long to move the Earth by the width of an atom, and if the Earth twitched, the kickback from the lever would fling him far and fast. The current crisis is about kickback from leverage in two places: households and financial services. Without leverage, downturns would be disappointments, but mortgages would not be foreclosed nor companies bankrupt. Leverage spreads the pain in ever-widening waves.

The way these dynamics played out is well known. US household debt started rising in the early 1980s, and its growth accelerated in 2001 (Exhibit 1). Leverage among Wall Street's five largest broker–dealers (Goldman Sachs, Merrill Lynch, Lehman Brothers, Bear Stearns, and Morgan Stanley) rose dramatically after 2004, when the US Securities and Exchange Commission exempted these firms from the long-standing 12-to-1 leverage ratio limit and let them regulate themselves. From 1990 to 2007, the whole financial-services sector expanded 2.5 times faster than overall GDP, and its profits rose from their 1947–96 average of 0.75 percent of GDP to 2.5 percent in 2007. Then falling

EXHIBIT 1

The runaway US consumer

Ratio of consumer debt to disposable income

Source: US Bureau of Economic Analysis; US Federal Reserve

home prices led to an unanticipated rise in foreclosure rates and a drop in the value of certain mortgage-backed securities. That decline quickly undid highly leveraged financial firms, whose failure spread loss and uncertainty throughout the system. US consumer spending continued at a high level through the first half of 2008 but by the third quarter had dropped at a 3.1 percent annualized rate. A recession—potentially a deep one—had arrived.

A structural break

Discerning the significance of these events is harder than recounting them. I think we are looking at a structural break with the past—a phrase from econometrics, where it denotes the moment in time-series data when trends and the patterns of associations among variables change.

A corporate crisis is often a sign that the company's business model has petered out—that the industry's underlying structure has changed dramatically, so old ways of doing business no longer work. In the 1990s, for instance, IBM's basic model of layering options and peripherals atop an integrated line of mainframe computers began to fail. Demand for computing was up, but IBM's way of providing it was down. Likewise, newspapers are now in crisis as the Internet grabs their readers and ads. Demand for information and analysis is increasing, but traditional publishing vehicles have difficulty making money from it.

The same principle applies to the economy as a whole. In most of the recessions of the past 40 years, demand caught up with capacity and growth returned in 10 to 18 months. This recession feels different because it is hard to imagine the full-steam reexpansion of financial services or a rapid turnaround in housing. Beyond these two hot spots, there seem to be unsustainable trends in commodity prices, oil imports, the nation's trade balance, the state of our schools, and large entitlement promises. Already, the idea that the United States can grow by borrowing money from China to finance consumption at home has begun to seem implausible. We know in our bones that the future will be different. When the business model of part or all of the economy shifts in this way, we can speak of a structural break.

Such a break often means hard times. Adjustment is neither easy nor quick. Difficult and volatile conditions wipe out some organizations—yet others prosper because they understand how to exploit the fact that old patterns vanish and new ones emerge. The first order of the day is to survive any downturns in the real economy (see sidebar, "Hard-times survival guide"), but the second is to benefit from these new patterns. A structural break is the very best time to be a strategist, for at the moment of change old sources of competitive advantage weaken and new sources appear. Afterward, upstarts can leap ahead of seemingly entrenched players.

In several industry sectors, the most recent structural break occurred in the 1980s, with the development of microprocessors, which led to much cheaper computing, personal and desktop computers, and the rise of a new kind of software industry. Those innovations begat the Internet and electronic commerce. More important for strategists, the break shifted the nature of competitive advantage dramatically. In 1985, for example, a telecom-equipment company needed sufficient scale to serve at least two of the three main continents—Asia, Europe, and North America—and skill at coordinating thousands of development engineers, manufacturing engineers, and workers. By 1995, firmware had become the primary source of advantage. Cisco Systems came out of nowhere to dominate its whole industry segment by deploying what at first was about 100,000 lines of elegant code written by a small team of talented people. That structural break allowed Silicon Valley's small-team culture to overtake Japan's advantages in industrial engineering and in managing a large, disciplined workforce. This shift in the logic of advantage changed the wealth of nations.

Structural breaks render obsolete many existing patterns of behavior, yet they point the way forward for some companies and at times even for whole economies. The Long Depression of 1893–97 marked the end of the railroad boom, for example, and the start of the transition to an economy based on sophisticated consumer goods. Milton Hershey built his early chocolate brand and distribution advantages in the middle of those hard times. GE was a product of the same period, for the structural break also marked the rise of a new economy based on electricity.

Although the 1930s were very hard times for the United States, not every industry or business declined. As the economy shifted massively from capital goods to consumer goods, some industries—such as steel, rubber, coal, glass, railroads, and building—suffered greatly, but consumer brands such as Kellogg's hit their stride. Campgrounds and motels blossomed along highways. Airline passenger traffic grew robustly. Entertainment surged with the growth of the radio and movie industries, and of their audience, during the Golden Age of Hollywood.

Likewise, during the decade from 1996 to 2005, overall consumer spending remained fairly flat in Japan. Still, the economy rotated into new things. The country, for example, has more than 200 brands of soft drinks, and each of Seven-Eleven Japan's small convenience stores carries more than 50 at any time. About 70 percent of these brands vanish each year and are replaced by new ones.

Many aspects of such structural changes will depend upon the government's policy response. Today, nuclear power, infrastructure repair, and fiber to the home are already on the list of possible stimuli for the

Hard-times survival guide

○ If you can't survive hard times, sell out early. Once you are in financial distress, you will have no bargaining power at all.

○ In hard times, save the core at the expense of the periphery. When times improve, recapture the periphery if it is still worthwhile.

○ Any stable source of good profits—any competitive advantage—attracts overhead, clutter, and cross-subsidies in good times. You can survive this kind of waste in such times. In hard times, you can't and must cut it.

○ If hard times have a good side, it's the pressure to cut expenses and find new efficiencies. Cuts and changes that raised interpersonal hackles in good times can be made in hard ones.

○ Use hard times to concentrate on and strengthen your competitive advantage. If you are confused about this concept, hard times will clarify it. Competitive advantage has two branches, both growing from the same root. You have a competitive advantage when you can take business away from another company at a profit and when your cash costs of doing business are low enough that you can survive in hard times.

○ Take advantage of hard times to buy the assets of distressed competitors at bargain-basement prices. The best assets are competitive advantages unwisely encumbered with debt and clutter.

○ In hard times, many suppliers are willing to renegotiate terms. Don't be shy.

○ In hard times, your buyers will want better terms. They might settle for rapid, reliable payments.

○ Focus on the employees and communities you will keep through the hard times. Good relations with people you have retained and helped will be repaid many times over when the good times return.

economy. In examining such business opportunities, it's important to recognize that competition for government funds is fierce. Nonetheless, the state can provide first-mover advantages in new growth areas. During Franklin Roosevelt's New Deal, for example, the federal government vastly expanded its record keeping. Since it needed something better than handwritten or typed notes, it turned to IBM's new-fangled punch card system. In the growth industry of aviation, Boeing lost its airline business as a result of the Air Mail Act of 1934 but also built substantial advantages by performing well on key military contracts.

The wrong way forward in a structural break during hard times is to try more of the same. The break and the hard times are sure indications that an old pattern has already been pushed to its limits and is destroying value. As an example of such a pattern, consider the financial sector's compensation incentives. Decades of careful research shows no evidence that anything but luck explains why some fund managers outperform others. Yet fund and even pension fund managers who supposedly outperform get huge pay and bonuses. Incentives are good in principle, but did Bear Stearns get competent risk management in return for the $4.4 billion bonus pool it distributed in 2006? Does any organization have to give its CEO a $40 million bonus to secure his services? If you pay people enough money to make any future payment beside the point, don't be surprised when they take vast long-term risks for short-term wins. In almost any pattern, overshooting produces negative returns.

Another pattern that may generate diminished or negative returns is the baffling complexity of our business and management systems. The financial-services industry is a poster child for the costs of this kind of complexity, as well. Calls to regulate such complex systems are misguided—regulators can't comprehend them if their creators don't. The best regulators can do in this case is to ban certain kinds of behavior.

Complexity also manifests itself in the soaring volume of e-mail. Philip Su, a Windows Vista software engineering manager, reports that the intensity of coordination on this project created "a phenomenon by which process engenders further process, eventually becoming a self-sustaining buzz."[1] We have all experienced this unanticipated side effect of apparently cheap communications. Unfortunately, lowering the cost of sending a message dramatically increases the amount of messaging. E-mail to a group of coworkers triggers immediate

[1] See Philip Su, "The world as best as I remember it," blogs.msdn.com/philipsu.

E X H I B I T 2

The rising cost of administration

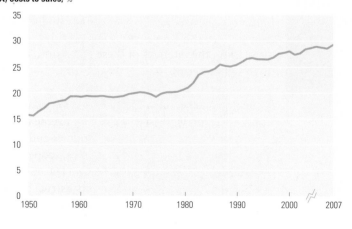

Share of selling, general, and administrative (SG&A) costs to sales, %

Source: Standard & Poor's

responses, the group of respondents expands, and responses proliferate like neutrons in a critical mass of plutonium. Messages are requests to do something, change something, or look at something. All that has a high cost. It was in the 1980s, as computing became a necessary part of the paraphernalia of management, that the percentage of pretax expenses accounted for by selling, general, and administrative costs (SG&A) began to accelerate (Exhibit 2).

In part, this rising administrative intensity shows the increasing importance of knowledge-based workers and the outsourcing of manual labor. It also reflects a more intense commitment to very complex systems comprising individual parts whose productivity is almost impossible to measure. Despite the claims of IT, marketing, and human resources that their programs generate strong returns on investment, corporations are betting on a whole approach to business, not on any one element. The risk is that in hard times, the system becomes the problem.

Consider an analogy. When oil is cheap and plentiful, we create a vast infrastructure that works well if oil remains cheap and plentiful. When it becomes expensive, we wish we had a different infrastructure. Similarly, when economic opportunities abound, we invest in a management infrastructure that harvests them very well. When the field of opportunities becomes less verdant, we must change our management infrastructure. A system that requires companies to spend at least $300,000 a year in wages, benefits, support personnel, and systems to enable one educated person to do his or her job could be unsustainable in a less luxuriant world.[2]

Doing things differently
It's hard to fix infrastructure when times are good and demand is growing. From 1993 to 1995, I served as director of INSEAD's Corporate Renewal Initiative, which studied and worked with companies trying to become more competitive. As business turned up in 1996, the interests of these companies flipped, as if by a switch, from reengineering to growth.

In the years since, most companies have indeed grown. They have also spent money on increasingly complex overhead structures to address the diversity of products and geographies and the demands of employees and governments. Now, in hard times, scope and variety will be cut, but costs won't automatically follow. The costs of managing scope and variety have been baked into the infrastructure—IT systems, sourcing systems, and processes for designing and marketing new products.

---

[2] As a baseline, US elementary and secondary educational systems spend about $250,000 a year on each class of average size (23 students). Another interesting data point: the US military spends $350,000 to $700,000 a year, depending on whose figures you believe, to put one soldier on the ground in Iraq.

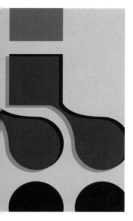

So during structural breaks in hard times, cutting costs isn't enough. Things have to be done differently, and on two levels: reducing the complexity of corporate structures and transforming business models. At the corporate level, the first commandment is to simplify and simplify again. Since companies must become more modular and diverse, eliminate coordinating committees, review boards, and other mechanisms connecting businesses, products, or geographies. The aim of these cuts is to provide lean central and support services that don't require business units to spend time and energy coordinating their activities. Break larger units into smaller ones to reveal cross-subsidies and to break political blockades. You may think that coordination costs will rise if you fragment the business, but you must do so to expose what ought to be streamlined.

Then start reforming individual businesses. There is a large and useful body of knowledge about how to go about doing so, and this is not the place to reprise it. In general terms, the first task is to understand how a business has survived, competed, and made money in the past. Don't settle for PowerPoint bar charts and graphs. If the business is too complex to comprehend, break it into comprehensible parts. Once you gain this critical understanding, you can start the work of reshaping. There is no magic formula. Reforming a business always takes insight and imagination.

In ordinary hard times, the traditional moves are reducing fixed costs, scope, and variety. But in hard times accompanied by structural breaks, you must rethink the way you manage. Companies that survive and go on to prosper look beyond costs to the detailed structure of managerial work. Several new issues come to the forefront:

- How much extra work results from the way incentive and evaluation systems relentlessly pressure managers to look busy and outperform one another?

- Which information flows can you omit? Information that doesn't inform value-creating decisions is a wasteful distraction.

- Which decisions and judgments can you standardize as policy rather than make in costly meetings and communications?

- How can you work with customers, suppliers, and the government to simplify their processes so that you can simplify yours?

We welcome your comments on this article. Please send them to quarterly_comments@ mckinsey.com.

Recessions are neither good for the economy nor morally uplifting. But since we are diving into a period of neck-snapping change, we had better start the process of reformation before it's too late. ◀

A fresh look at strategy under uncertainty:
An interview

Although even the highest levels of uncertainty don't prevent businesses from analyzing predicaments rationally, says author Hugh Courtney, the financial crisis has shown us the limits of our tools—and minds.

Hugh Courtney's book *20/20 Foresight: Crafting Strategy in an Uncertain World* was published the day before the terrorist attacks of September 11, 2001. As the economist and former McKinsey associate principal recalls, in the following weeks interviewers often asked him, "Does this change everything? Is this stuff still valid? The world is so much more uncertain." Says Courtney, "The honest answer then was that the only thing that had changed was our perception of risks and uncertainties that were always there. And it's the same answer I give today about the current global business and financial situation."

One of Courtney's contributions to the literature of strategy was a four-part framework to help managers determine the level of uncertainty surrounding strategic decisions (exhibit). In level one, there is a clear, single view of the future; in level two, a limited set of possible future outcomes, one of which will occur; in level three, a range of possible future outcomes; and in level four, a limitless range of possible future outcomes. Courtney, an associate dean of executive programs and professor of the practice of strategy at the University of Maryland's Robert H. Smith School of Business, discussed the relevance of this idea in a recent interview with the *Quarterly*.

The *Quarterly*: *How do you evaluate the level of business uncertainty today?*

Hugh Courtney: The financial crisis has actually brought greater clarity because it has forced us to recognize that we have a lot more level three and level four situations than we would have admitted a few months ago. They probably were there all along, yet the bias was toward thinking that issues were more at level one and level two. Specifically, we have learned how interdependent our financial markets are and how systemic failure in any important node of the network can work very rapidly through the system and bring liquidity to a halt. So our scenarios about the availability of capital around the world have changed significantly.

Maybe the world and the uncertainties we face haven't changed all that much as a result of the financial crisis, but our perception of risks has. That means there is a real opportunity to rethink the way we make strategic decisions, the way we plan under uncertainty. We should realize that, across sectors, for most important decisions we're actually pretty far to the right—levels three and four—in the uncertainty spectrum.

The *Quarterly*: *What does that mean in practice for managers?*

Hugh Courtney: Level four situations are, by definition, ones for which you can't really bound the range of outcomes, because it's anybody's guess. I'm sure we've all felt a little bit of that in the last few months. So the question is, do you just have to wing it? Is that what strategic decision making comes down to? I don't think that's true at all, but level four does require a different mind-set.

EXHIBIT

The four levels of residual uncertainty

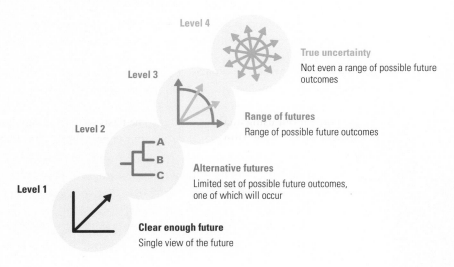

Level 4

True uncertainty
Not even a range of possible future outcomes

Level 3

Range of futures
Range of possible future outcomes

Level 2

A
B
C

Alternative futures
Limited set of possible future outcomes, one of which will occur

Level 1

Clear enough future
Single view of the future

Hugh Courtney

From level one to level three, the presumption is that you can do some bottom-up analysis. You can figure out what the value drivers are and do some market research and some competitive intelligence. All this may not give you a precise forecast, but you'll be able to bound the outcomes somehow. That's impossible in level four situations, by definition. There's just stuff that's fundamentally unknowable—truly an ambiguous world.

On the other hand, that doesn't mean you can't be rigorous in thinking through strategic decisions in level four. It just requires you to work backward from potential strategies to what you would have to believe about the future for those strategies to succeed. The classic example would be biotech—early-stage biotech investments have always faced level four uncertainty, because you're playing with therapies with an ultimate commercial viability that is unknown.

The *Quarterly*: *What advice would you give to a chief strategy officer today?*

Hugh Courtney: I would start with, "What were you doing in strategic planning before the financial crisis hit?" and "How well do you think it worked?" As I said, what's changed is largely our perception of uncertainty. Most CSOs would reply, "Well, we had a pretty standard strategic-planning process. We did some industry analysis and market research and tried to do some long-term discounted cash flow on our opportunities. It was very financially driven and we felt it worked pretty well." In the end, though, you would probably find that they were treating a lot of level three and four issues like level one and two issues and relying on the wrong tool kit.

So I would start with scenario-planning techniques—even though scenario planning has been around for decades, it's still a niche tool in strategic-development and -planning efforts. The CSO and I would also talk about using analogies better. The basis of the analogy doesn't have to be the exact thing you've done in the past, but it should be a similar space, geography, or basic business model that you can learn from. Many people today are asking what might be analogous situations, such as the Great Depression or the 1997 Asian financial crisis, and I really understand why they are focused on them: it's a classic example of using level four reasoning when it's hard to use any other.

Finally, this is a good time to rethink your planning process. Have you been doing strategic planning on an annual basis as a paper-pushing

exercise? That will have to change. In the months to come, you're going to have to make decisions very quickly on fundamental opportunities that may drive your earnings performance for the next decade or more, and you've got to be prepared to make these decisions in real time. That requires a continuous focus on market and competitive intelligence and far more frequent conversations—daily, if necessary—among the top team about the current situation. Senior executives already may be in closer contact because of the emergency they face, but that doesn't necessarily imply that they have the raw material and the structure to work through strategic decisions systematically. These daily conversations have to move beyond getting through that day's crisis to more fundamental strategic issues as well, because the decisions made today may open up or close off opportunities for months and years to come.

The *Quarterly*: *How has your thinking changed since you wrote 20/20 Foresight?*

Hugh Courtney: The financial crisis and 9/11 are wake-up calls to think about better management of risk and uncertainty. I find myself these days taking uncertainly more seriously. Remember, in the book I wrote that everyone should take uncertainty seriously, but day to day I fall into standard patterns that behavioral scientists have described— for example, I tend to have too much confidence in my ability to predict the future.

In the aftermath of the financial crisis, I've been thinking a lot about how these fundamental human cognitive biases influence everything we do in strategy development. We actually know more about the world today than we did a few months ago, because there's information in the meltdown. But the message behind that information is really, "You fools, remember that you're human." Remember the biases that lead us to be overconfident in our ability to forecast the future. Remember that the most important decisions for most companies will truly be level three and, many times, level four decisions. Our standard strategic-planning tool kits—the ones that we are most comfortable with and that we learn in MBA programs—don't do a really good job for that.

So we ought to pay attention to this wake-up call. Embrace uncertainty. Get to know it. In uncertainty lies great opportunity. If you don't try to understand what's separating the known from the unknown from the unknowable, you're really missing out. You're just playing roulette with big money—usually other people's money. It behooves us to take uncertainty seriously and to fundamentally rethink the way we do strategic thinking and planning.

The full version of this interview is available on mckinseyquarterly.com.

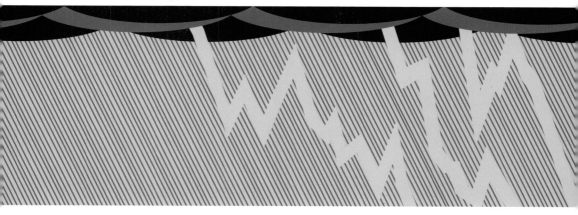

Taking improbable events seriously:

An interview with the author of *The Black Swan*

Nassim Nicholas Taleb explains why the rarity
and unpredictability of certain events does not make
them unimportant.

The scholar, trader, and author **Nassim Nicholas Taleb** brings a
decidedly contrarian view to the world of finance, statistics, and risk.
In 2007, he published *The Black Swan: The Impact of the Highly
Improbable*, which argues that we should never ignore the possibility
or importance of rare, unpredictable events. In this interview with
the *Quarterly*, he looks at the current financial crisis through the lens
of his *Black Swan* thinking.

The *Quarterly*: *For people who haven't read* The Black Swan, *can
you quickly summarize what they should know to understand your
point of view on recent events in global financial markets?*

Nassim Nicholas Taleb: Before Europeans discovered Australia,
we had no reason to believe that swans could be any other color but
white. But they discovered Australia, saw black swans, and revised
their beliefs. My idea in *The Black Swan* is to make people think of the
unknown and of the potency of the unknown, particularly a certain
class of events that you can't imagine but can cost you a lot: rare but
high-impact events.

So my black swan doesn't have feathers. My black swan is an event
with three properties. Number one, its probability is low, based on past
knowledge. Two, although its probability is low, when it happens it

Nassim Nicholas Taleb

has a massive impact. And three, people don't see it coming before the fact, but after the fact, everybody saw it coming. So it's prospectively unpredictable but retrospectively predictable.

Now that we're in this financial crisis, for example, everybody saw it coming. But did they own bank stocks? Yes, they did. In other words, they say that they saw it coming because they had some thoughts in the shower about this possibility—not because they truly took measures to protect themselves from it.

These things have a life of their own. You cannot predict a black swan. We also have some psychological blindness to black swans. We don't understand them, because, genetically, we did not evolve in an environment where there were a lot of black swans. It's not part of our intuition.

The Quarterly: *Say a little more about the relationship between black swans and the global financial crisis.*

Nassim Nicholas Taleb: I warned in *The Black Swan* against some classes of risk people don't understand and against the tools used by risk managers—tools that could not fully capture the properties of the world in which we live. The financial crisis took place because people took a lot of hidden risks, which meant that a small blip could have massive consequences.

The Quarterly: *You question many of the underpinnings of modern financial theory. If you were the dean of a business school, how would you overhaul the curriculum?*

Nassim Nicholas Taleb: I would tell people to learn more accounting, more computer science, more business history, more financial history. And I would ban portfolio theory immediately. It's what caused the problems. Frankly, anything in finance that has equations is suspicious. I would also ban the use of statistics because unless you know statistics very, very well, it's a dangerous, double-edged sword. And I would ban linear regression. All these things don't work.

The Quarterly: *What are your concerns with statistics and portfolio theory?*

Nassim Nicholas Taleb: The field of statistics is based on something called the law of large numbers: as you increase your sample size, no single observation is going to hurt you. Sometimes that works. But the rules are based on classes of distribution that don't always hold in our world.

All statistics come from games. But our world doesn't resemble games. We don't have dice that can deliver. Instead of dice with one through six, the real world can have one through five—and then a trillion. The real world can do that. In the 1920s, the German mark went from three marks to a dollar to three trillion to a dollar in no time.

That's why portfolio theory simply doesn't work. It uses metrics like variance to describe risk, while most real risk comes from a single observation, so variance is a volatility that doesn't really describe the risk. It's very foolish to use variance.

The *Quarterly*: *What does all this mean for managers at nonfinancial companies? What should they be doing differently?*

Nassim Nicholas Taleb: I recommend two things. Number one, take the maximum amount of risk and other forms of exposure to positive black swans when this costs you very little if you're wrong and earns you a lot if you're right. Number two, minimize your exposure to negative black swans.

This is exactly the opposite of what the banks did. They had no real upside and a lot of downside—or, to be more precise, they got a little bit of cash flow to have all the downside. I recommend the opposite. Be hyperconservative when it comes to downside risk, hyperaggressive when it comes to opportunities that cost you very little. Most people have the wrong instinct. They do the opposite.

The *Quarterly*: *You're also a critic of scenario planning. Is there a way to do it effectively?*

We welcome your comments on this article. Please send them to quarterly_comments@ mckinsey.com.

Nassim Nicholas Taleb: I don't like scenario planning, because people don't think out of the box. So scenario planning may focus on four, five, or six scenarios that you can envision, at the expense of others you can't. Instead of looking at scenarios and forecasts, you should be looking to see how fragile your portfolio is. How vulnerable are you to model error? How vulnerable is your cash flow to changes in any parameter of your calculations? My idea is to base your navigation on fragility.

The full version of this interview is available on mckinseyquarterly.com.

Creative destruction and the financial crisis:

An interview with
Richard Foster

A coauthor of *Creative Destruction* explains how the business world—and the capitalist system—will change in the aftermath of the financial crisis.

Richard Foster, a McKinsey director from 1982 to 2004, is a coauthor of *Creative Destruction: Why Companies That Are Built to Last Underperform the Market—and How to Successfully Transform Them.* In that book, he and Sarah Kaplan argue that to endure, companies must embrace what economist Joseph Schumpeter called "creative destruction" and change at the pace and scale of the capital markets, without losing control over current operations. In a recent interview with the *Quarterly*, Foster offered his view of how the current financial crisis might change the business world and the capitalist system.

The *Quarterly*: *How does your vision of creative destruction apply to today's situation?*

Richard Foster: Let's start by looking back. In the 1970s, we had the "Nifty 50"—invulnerable companies that couldn't possibly lose, and of course they all did. It will be the same today; there will be surprising losers, and survival will come down to simple things, like cash and margins. If you're a low-margin company without a lot of cash or perhaps with too much leverage, you will not make it. Someone will figure out how to do better.

In the financial-services sector, the upheaval will create a new generation of leaders. Fifty years ago, we didn't have 8,000 hedge fund managers. Then somebody said, "We can go short as well as long; we have much better information than people did in the 1930s, and the information comes to us instantaneously rather than days after the event. We can make a lot of money modeling and leveraging that information." So the hedge funds were born. How many of those guys had been successful at mutual-fund management? I don't think any. They might have been commodity traders, but few were mutual-fund managers. Today, other kinds of people with no experience or expertise will challenge incumbents from outside the industry, and there will be a lot of them. Most of the challengers will fail, but a few will succeed, and they'll become the heroes of the next generation. If you had to bet on anything, that's it because that's what has happened in the past.

The *Quarterly*: *Could you elaborate on this life cycle?*

Richard Foster: In the book, Sarah Kaplan and I show that over the long term, the market performs better than companies do. There can be periods—5, 7, 10, even 15 years—when that isn't the case, but corporate performance always reverts to a lower level than the market because the economy is changing at a faster pace and on a larger scale than any individual company so far has been able to do without losing control. That's the challenge: to create, operate, and trade—to divest old businesses and acquire or build new businesses—at the pace and scale of the market without losing control.

The balance among creating, trading, and excelling operationally changes over time. When the economy is in a growth spurt, there's more creating. Few companies are trading very much and operations are fine. In those circumstances, the newer companies in the economy tend to outperform the index, and the older companies that are only focused on operations underperform the market.

As the market collapses, the weaker upstarts get squeezed out. The survivors are the cash-rich "operators," which perform at levels closer to the averages, which themselves are lower. Companies that operate well shine in down times, as they are now. Every investor on the planet is looking for companies that have cash left. The turmoil will clear away the weaker companies—the companies that have taken too much risk. This doesn't mean they're bad companies; it's just that they've taken on too much risk given their balance sheet resources.

The *Quarterly*: *What happens then?*

Richard Foster: New, young companies that have conserved cash and have solid and often expanding margins surge ahead. When this happened in the '70s, companies such as The Limited, The Gap, Home Depot, and John Malone's TeleCommunications Inc. sprung from the burned forest. After the crash of 1987, Microsoft, Oracle, and Amgen

Richard Foster

took off. Then in the '90s, we had the Internet companies. Creation will happen again and will again leave behind the big guys trying to rely solely on operations.

The *Quarterly*: *To what extent is today's financial crisis different from earlier ones?*

Richard Foster: The granddaddy of cycles in this economy is the equity premium, which is the difference between the longer-term total returns to shareholders and the supposedly risk-free debt rate. It is the premium the equity investor gets for taking the equity risk. Looking back, we can see seven great cycles. During the boom times, when the equity premium goes way too high, everybody hocks everything to get in on the game, and this creates the conditions for a crash. When the crash occurs, the politicians come in and say it was this or that person's fault. Then they create regulatory institutions, and virtually every one of those institutions—starting with the Federal Reserve, in 1913, as a result of the crash of 1907—has been quite productive for the nation in the longer term. This includes the formation of the Securities and Exchange Commission, in 1934; the Investment Company Act, in 1940; the beginning of the end of fixed commission rates in 1970; and the Sarbanes–Oxley Act, in the early 2000s.

The *Quarterly*: *What happens in the aftermath of the new regulations?*

Richard Foster: What do self-respecting entrepreneurs do when subjected to new regulations? They learn the regulations backward and forward and then vow never to start another business that falls within the scope of those regulations. And so off the entrepreneur goes to find a new way. That's one reason credit default swaps eventually took the form they did—the other options were regulated.

The new entrepreneur often seeks ways to innovate outside the scope of the newly established regulations. In the beginning, all that works out fine. We have innovations, we love the people who created them, they're great heroes, the returns are strong, everybody says, "I'm going to be one of those guys." Eventually, all the truly good guys who are going to get into that business have done so. The opportunity starts drawing less savory figures—charlatans who overmarket, cut corners, establish usurious contracts, and do other clever things to generate profit for themselves. They end up bringing the system down. Then guess what happens? At the end of that period, after the equity premium has soared and collapsed again, the government steps in and regulates the systems, this time focusing on the last wave of abuse. And then we start over.

We were getting somewhat better at handling these cycles until 2000, but since then we've gotten worse. The collapse of 2008 isn't like the crash of 1929, because we have the institutions that were created in the last century, and they are very effective. Understanding the differences between the '30s and today is at least as important as understanding the similarities.

*The **Quarterly**: Capitalism has just taken a beating. What will the future look like?*

Richard Foster: The essence of capitalism is capitalizing—bringing forward the future value of cash to the present so that society can grow more quickly by taking risks. It goes back to the Dutchmen in the 16th century, sitting at their coffeehouses in Amsterdam and Leiden, loaning each other money for a guaranteed return. Someone said, "I'll give you a little higher return if you give me a piece of the action"—and equity was invented. That had the effect of bringing forward, into real cash today, the net present value of future earnings. That levered society and allowed it to grow at a much higher rate than it would otherwise have. Equity was a very clever invention, and we are not going to give it up. This is the way people are. This is the way commerce works and will continue to work unless capitalism ends. And that won't happen, regardless of what you read in the press.

55
Freeing
up cash from
operations

58
Maintaining
the customer
experience

61
Upgrading
talent

64
Managing IT
spending

Smart cost cutting in the downturn

Is it possible to cut costs in a way that positions a company for success after the downturn? The articles that follow look at how to achieve that alluring but elusive goal in operations, customer service, talent management, and information technology.

Freeing up cash from operations

As the credit crunch slows the economy, companies shouldn't make cuts across the board; in fact, tough times can actually make it easier to improve operations.

Alexander Niemeyer and Bruce Simpson

Alexander Niemeyer is a principal in McKinsey's Miami office, and **Bruce Simpson** is a director in the Toronto office.

In 1999, a major North American company with 80 regionally oriented divisions launched an effort to enhance its operational effectiveness. Pilot programs in select markets achieved 10 to 15 percent cost reductions, while increasing sales by more than 15 percent. On the heels of this success, the company trained more than 25 "change agents" to roll out the program. Then a recession hit, and executives in the company's headquarters got nervous. In their search for quick savings opportunities, they fired the change agents and asked each of the 80 divisions to continue on its own. A year later, as performance deteriorated, a major private-equity firm acquired the company. Although the firm tried to reinstate the improvement efforts, the capacity and appetite for thoughtful change had evaporated, and the company endured four years of zero profit and sales growth.

The company's experience typifies the kind of mistakes companies can make as they slash costs during downturns (see sidebar, "Budgeting on autopilot"). During the 2001–02 recession, for example, some were quick to cut operational overhead. These cuts made it challenging for executives to manage day-to-day execution and service or plan for further performance improvements that would enable them to emerge from the recession successfully. Similarly, during the last recession, the dissolution of lean performance or Six Sigma groups was common.

Some companies believed they lacked the time or money to see operational-improvement efforts through and opted instead for across-the-board head count reductions of, say, 10 percent. This approach was risky: it led companies to squander investments in people and process improvements. More important, companies struggled to restart these efforts, because workers no longer believed that their leaders cared about "doing things the right way," and the disillusionment undermined the integrity of operations efforts.

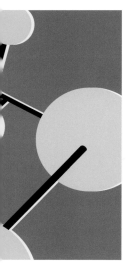

It's easy to spot these mistakes in retrospect. But how, in the heat of battle, as a credit crunch slows economic activity, can companies avoid the impulse simply to batten down their operations and ride out the storm? Can companies systematically cut the fat—not the muscle—while building the future as well? Can they be creative rather than reactive? Yes. But only if senior executives frequently and visibly emphasize a balanced view of the company's operations. In practice, this will probably mean taking short-term steps to keep cash flows healthy. That will help executives gain the flexibility to continue supporting longer-term efforts to improve operational capabilities and performance, whether these are in manufacturing, purchasing, supply chain management, or product development.

Except in recessions, most companies don't pay enough attention to cash, since its impact on earnings isn't immediate. As a result, many enterprises have solid opportunities to free up cash and reduce or postpone spending it. One obvious move is to tighten the management of accounts payable and receivable: taking simple steps, such as enforcing payment terms and sending bills early, can often add two to four days of sales to cash—the equivalent of an additional $100 million to $200 million for a typical consumer goods manufacturer with $20 billion in sales.

And there are great opportunities in the guts of a company's operations. Many companies, for example, can quickly and safely convert significant amounts of inventory into cash. Of course, there are more and less effective ways to tackle inventory. In our experience, asking the CFO to set reduction targets can have service implications that damage customer relationships. Instead, operations and sales leaders should review their inventories more systematically and eliminate the extra buffers that every step in the supply chain tends to add. (We all know the rationale: "I add 10 percent to my forecast"; "I assume it takes seven days to get here, just to be safe"; "I order a week early, just in case.") An approach like this can usually reduce inventories by 20 percent. For our $20 billion consumer goods company, a reduction of this magnitude could approach $400 million— enough to cover a 2 percent decline in revenue for the year.

Budgeting on autopilot

Dan Lovallo

Dan Lovallo is a professor at the University of Sydney and an adviser to McKinsey.

During downturns, many multidivisional companies cut costs by some arbitrary fraction across all business units. Similarly, during times of economic and industry growth, budgets often increase by an arbitrary percentage of sales or assets. In fact, for diversified companies in the United States, the correlation of the year-to-year percentage of investments going to each business unit from 1985 to 2005 is 0.85; in other words, each business unit's share of the investment pie remained fairly constant over time. This correlation holds up during good times and bad.

Such behavior makes a certain psychological and organizational sense—it taps into our human notions of fairness, is cognitively simple, and raises few political concerns. As a practical matter, all executives are capable of making such across-the-board increases and decreases in the very short term. Thoughtful executives, however, should quickly focus on more granular growth and profitability differentials within business units in order to trim underperforming investments dramatically while simultaneously seeding promising ones for the coming spring. This is an important insight in normal conditions and an even more crucial one during these tough economic times, when widening the gap between your company and the crowd becomes urgent.

We welcome your comments on this article. Please send them to quarterly_comments@ mckinsey.com.

Similarly, many companies can drastically cut capital spending. The best way to do this is not to impose artificial cutoffs but to assemble the relevant, knowledgeable parties to look for ways of postponing or reducing capital project spending and to exploit the current willingness of major project suppliers to renegotiate prices. These kinds of collaborative efforts can reduce capital spending by 20 percent and can delay an additional 30 percent in 12 months. For the hypothetical packaged-goods manufacturer, that would free up $500 million in cash this year.

Increasing cash flows in these ways is far preferable to alternative, slash-and-burn approaches involving indiscriminate head count reductions that often generate dissatisfied employees and customers, as well as service failures. What's more, the extra cash should give executives peace of mind about continuing to focus on long-term efforts to build operational capabilities and improve performance. And there might even be a silver lining in the cloud hanging over the global economy: the tough environment may help companies overcome the mind-set barriers that slow down so many improvement efforts, while at the same time creating opportunities for thoughtful, practical, and creative leaders to thrive.

Maintaining the customer experience

Stinting on customer service is a common and sometimes costly response to tough economic times. By managing the customer experience more rigorously, companies can maintain quality while still saving money.

Adam Braff and John C. DeVine

The challenging economy is putting consumer companies such as airlines, banks, and retailers in the difficult position of cutting back the service levels that customers have come to expect in recent years. These companies are closing retail locations, reducing hours of operation, and making do with less staff in stores and call centers. Meanwhile, faced with rising costs, they are also increasing prices, either overtly or through fees. As a result, our customer experience research shows that satisfaction scores are reversing the upward trend of the past few years and actually dropping in a number of industries.

So it's not surprising that most executives think compromising service levels is a mistake. When we interviewed senior executives from 11 leading service delivery companies, all but one agreed that improving the customer experience is growing in importance to their companies, customers, and competitors.

How can consumer businesses make necessary investments in service while facing the pressure on revenues and costs? Our review of the companies with the best customer service records in ten industries suggests that one key is to minimize wasteful spending while learning to invest in the drivers of satisfaction. Specifically, companies should challenge their beliefs about service and test those beliefs analytically. Many will discover that long-held but seldom-reviewed assertions about what customers really want are wrong.

Adam Braff is a principal in McKinsey's Washington, DC, office, and **John DeVine** is a principal in the Seattle office.

Consider service levels, specifically average time-to-answer, which is one of the most common metrics used in call centers. Service levels—often based on regulation or historical precedent—are set by call-center managers and then used to calculate staffing requirements. But service levels are challenging to maintain and costly to improve: raising them by 10 percent requires much more than a 10 percent increase in staff.

Companies that closely manage the customer experience have taken a rigorous approach to resetting service levels and, in some cases, are saving money without degrading them or customer satisfaction. In short, these companies have carefully measured the "breakpoints" to find their customers' true sensitivity to service level changes. One company, a wireless telecommunications services provider, found that its customers had two breakpoints at X and Y seconds on a call; answering the phone immediately (less than X seconds) produced delight, while leaving customers on hold for longer (more than Y seconds) produced strong dissatisfaction (exhibit). Although customers were fairly indifferent to service levels between X and Y, the company's average time to answer was only loosely managed between these two points.

The company considered raising service levels to the "delight breakpoint" or reducing them to just above the "patience threshold."

EXHIBIT

The breaking point

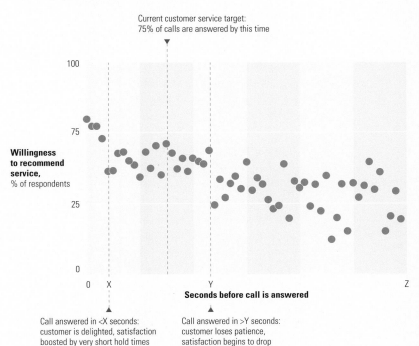

Disguised example of a wireless-telecommunications company

Current customer service target:
75% of calls are answered by this time

100

75

Willingness to recommend service,
% of respondents

25

0

0 X   Y   Z
Seconds before call is answered

Call answered in <X seconds:
customer is delighted, satisfaction
boosted by very short hold times

Call answered in >Y seconds:
customer loses patience,
satisfaction begins to drop

Customer-lifetime-value economics pointed to the second option: relaxing service levels but guarding against crossing the patience threshold. The drop in customer satisfaction was negligible, but the savings in staffing were significant, and the company ended up saving more than $7 million annually—much of which was reinvested in improvements to its problem-resolution process.

This scenario isn't an isolated example. The same principles apply to setting up a new account, scheduling an appointment, answering a nonurgent e-mail, or having customers wait in line. In our experience, most companies that analyze their service levels carefully find that some wait times have become more important to customers than others and that overstaffing to hit service targets that customers don't care about is costing them money.

A second variety of overinvestment that we often see involves capital and technology. In one example, a bank scrutinized a costly ATM upgrade aimed at improving the user interface and adding screening barriers around the machines to enhance user privacy. An analysis showed that the equipment was moderately important (driving 5 percent of overall satisfaction). Yet more mundane factors—the existence of enough ATMs and the consistent availability of cash in all machines—were not only about 50 percent more important to customers but also perceived by customers as a bigger problem for the bank. Consequently, the bank pulled the plug on its capital plan for ATM upgrades and redirected those funds into addressing accessibility issues and cash-out conditions.

Other good places to look for potential overinvestment include marketing campaigns (for example, offering to move a customer to a cheaper rate plan regardless of whether the customer says cost is a problem) and excessive use of bill credits and adjustments. The business case for these "customer delight treatments" can include unrealistic assumptions about how they will increase customer referrals and retention. And often, there is no business case.

Finding these savings requires rigor in customer experience analytics: the collection of customer-level data, matching survey responses to actual behavior, and statistical analysis that differentiates to the extent possible between correlation and causation. It also requires a willingness to question long-held internal beliefs reinforced through repetition by upper management. The executive in charge of the customer experience needs to have the courage to raise these questions, along with the instinct to look for ways to self-fund customer experience improvements. Sophisticated companies that figure out what matters most to customers, eliminate the investments that don't matter, and finance the ones that do will thrive—and may find themselves, when the economy returns to normal, with fewer competitors. ▼

We welcome your comments on this article. Please send them to quarterly_comments@ mckinsey.com.

Upgrading talent

A downturn can give smart companies a chance to upgrade their talent.

Matthew Guthridge, John R. McPherson, and William J. Wolf

Downturns place companies' talent strategies at risk. As deteriorating performance forces increasingly aggressive head count reductions, it's easy to lose valuable contributors inadvertently, damage morale or the company's external reputation among potential employees, or drop the ball on important training and staff-development programs. But there is a better way. By emphasizing talent in cost-cutting efforts, employers can intelligently strengthen the value proposition they offer current and potential employees and position themselves strongly for growth when economic conditions improve.

Companies can maintain their attractiveness to internal and external talent by using cost-cutting efforts as an opportunity to redesign jobs so that they become more engaging for the people undertaking them. A job's level of responsibility, degree of autonomy, and span of control all contribute to employee satisfaction. Head count reductions provide a powerful incentive to use existing resources better by breaking down silos and increasing the span of control for challenging managerial roles—thus improving the odds of engaging key talent in the redesigned jobs.

Matthew Guthridge is an associate principal in McKinsey's London office, John McPherson is a director in the Dallas office, and William Wolf is a principal in the Washington, DC, office.

Consider Cisco Systems' approach to downsizing during the last recession. In 2001, as deteriorating financial performance forced the elimination of 8,500 jobs, Cisco redesigned roles and responsibilities to improve cross-functional alignment and reduce duplication.[1] The more collaborative environment fostered by such moves increased workplace satisfaction and productivity for many employees. Initiatives like Cisco's succeed when companies focus on redesigning jobs and retaining talent at the outset of downsizing efforts.

In addition to redesigning roles, companies cutting jobs should carefully protect training and development programs. These are not only essential to maintaining workplace morale and increasing long-term productivity, but they also give people the skills necessary to carry out redesigned jobs that have greater spans of control. During the last recession, International Paper continued offering classes at its leadership institute by replacing external facilitators with the company's senior leaders.[2] This approach not only reduced the cost of delivery but also, thanks to the involvement of senior leaders, redirected the content of the leadership program by tying it more closely to decisions and skills affecting the company's current performance. Similarly, IBM retained its employee-development programs during its major performance challenges in the mid- to late 1980s. It took the arrival of Lou Gerstner as CEO and a new strategy to turn the company around, but the historical investments IBM had made in developing its people helped achieve a successful turnaround.

Before undertaking widespread layoffs, companies should use their performance-management processes to help identify strong employees. Companies that conduct disciplined, meritocratic assessments of performance and potential are well placed to make good personnel decisions. These companies should also bring additional strategic considerations to the decisions. They should assess which types of talent drive business value today and which will drive it three years from now, as well as which talent segments are currently available and which will be in the future—keeping in mind, for example, that new MBAs will be equally available in two years. They should also look at which types of talent would take years to replace or develop— for instance, skilled electric utility engineers in an environment where retirements are dramatically reducing supply. Performance management well informed by key strategic questions can minimize the negative cultural impact of downsizing, improve the bottom line, and help identify talented people the company should try to retain.

Companies that are reducing staff must focus relentlessly on the internal cultural and external reputational implications of cost-cutting efforts. Although strong employer brands are resilient, it's difficult to reestablish brand strength once the culture has been damaged. The way many companies conduct large-scale downsizing decreases

[1] See Victoria Chang, Jennifer Chatman, and Charles O'Reilly, "Developing a human capital strategy," *California Management Review*, 2005, Volume 47, Number 2, pp. 137–67.
[2] See Jessica Marquez, "Ready for recession," *Workforce Management*, April 7, 2008.

efficiency, morale, and motivation on the part of remaining employees. It also increases voluntary turnover among high performers and compromises a company's ability to attract strong talent in the future, as potential employees wonder how risky it is to take a job there.

Counteracting these tendencies requires creativity. In 2001, Cisco gave generous severance packages and assistance with job searches to the workers it laid off and launched a program that paid one-third of salary, plus benefits and stock options, to ex-employees who agreed to work for a local charity or community organization. Steps like these protected Cisco's employer brand by attempting to make departing employees feel better about Cisco and underscored the company's commitment to its people for those who remained. The results were measurable: employee satisfaction remained high, and Cisco retained a prominent spot on *Fortune* magazine's "Best Companies to Work For" list.

A strong employer brand is also important for companies undertaking selective recruitment even as they cut personnel costs elsewhere. Using slowdowns to uncover and hire displaced talent is often fruitful. Studies have shown that although overall levels of recruitment may level off or even fall, the quality of workers hired rises in recessions.[3] And opportunities to find and hire displaced talent may be particularly valuable during this downturn, as massive downsizing in the financial-services sector makes available to nonfinancial companies a large pool of highly educated and motivated professionals who previously might not have considered jobs outside their previous employers or industries.

Some organizations are moving surprisingly quickly in response to these opportunities in the talent market. In late October 2008, the US Internal Revenue Service hosted a Manhattan career fair targeted at displaced financial-services professionals. More than 1,300 people attended, many standing in line for three hours to learn more about an employer that offered a newly interesting brand of "job stability."

We welcome your comments on this article. Please send them to quarterly_comments@ mckinsey.com.

Cost cutting during a downturn is often necessary to ensure a company's current profitability and future competitiveness. Rather than freezing all hiring and employee-development programs, companies should use this period as an opportunity to upgrade talent and better engage existing staff. This means reinvesting a percentage of the capital liberated from cost cutting into, for example, selective recruiting and development programs and in efforts to safeguard the culture and to redesign jobs so that they are more engaging to the remaining employees.

[3]See Paul J. Devereux, "Occupational upgrading and the business cycle," *Labour*, 2002, Volume 16, Number 3, pp. 423–52.

Managing IT spending

Many IT organizations will reduce their spending
in 2009. A strong management focus can mitigate
the pain—and create opportunities.

James M. Kaplan and Johnson Sikes

With growth slowing and valuations declining, businesses badly need
to extract value from their IT functions. The operative questions
are, "How much?" and "How?" As CIOs choose a path, they need
to determine whether they can afford to take a "through cycle"
perspective, balancing short-term financial improvements and the possible impact on longer-term capabilities. They must also consider
the need to act quickly to generate cash, even if such moves prove less
attractive once the recession ends.

Almost all IT organizations can and should reduce IT spending in
2009. But this will be difficult. Many companies have built up complex
application environments that require ongoing support. Contractual
commitments to vendors can be difficult to modify. Adding to the challenge, organizations rarely agree internally on business priorities
for IT.

Still, with sufficient management focus, it's possible to cut costs dramatically and quickly. Companies can trim and rationalize demand for
new applications. Existing IT capacity, like servers and storage, can
be shared and application maintenance spending capped. Taking a "zero
based" view of an organization (reimagining it from scratch) may
help to peel away unnecessary management layers and eliminate non-
value-adding functions. Meanwhile, companies can renegotiate some

James Kaplan is a
principal in McKinsey's
New York office, where
Johnson Sikes is a
consultant.

contracts to reflect changing market conditions and can accelerate efforts to move operations offshore.

Some businesses, however, face tougher challenges. They must substantially improve their cash positions just to survive. As they cut near-term costs, these IT groups will need to reduce investments and rationalize organizations aggressively. One company in danger of violating debt covenants reduced its IT cash outlays by 22 percent in a year, excluding severance. It made tough choices about which capabilities for which business units would be delayed and what kind of new, lower levels of IT service would be acceptable.

Making money from assets is another path for those needing to generate cash. All large organizations have hundreds of millions of dollars locked up in IT assets. They may consider selling data centers or spinning off overseas service centers. Sale–leaseback transactions of such facilities are another option. Even if these moves could be unfavorable in the longer term, the short-term value of cash may make them necessary.

Companies that face less severe capital constraints and can navigate through the recession cycle should not only cut costs but also seek out additional opportunities to improve business performance. They can use IT to increase revenues and reduce operational costs in the short term. Often, these improvements can be made with modest investments. Companies can use data more effectively and optimize processes through technology. IT, for example, can be vital to improving supply chains by enhancing logistics and inventory management. Similarly, better data can sharpen insights into customer segments, pinpointing opportunities to change prices or focus sales efforts. Over 12 to 18 months, these projects may return up to ten times the bottom-line impact of simple IT cost reductions.

We welcome your comments on this article. Please send them to quarterly_comments@ mckinsey.com.

Companies with sufficient management resources in this downturn may want to undertake more far-reaching restructuring of their IT departments. In many areas, IT functions can realize further efficiencies by changing management practices and models and promoting more interaction with the rest of the business. Improving IT's cash situation in the short term can, in many cases, generate funding and support within the organization for more far-reaching improvements that will have even broader impact. ▼

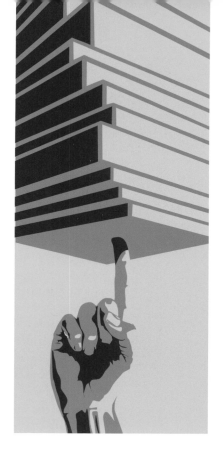

The downturn's new rules for marketers

The old recession playbook won't work this time around.

David Court

David Court is a director in McKinsey's Dallas office.

Around the world, marketing and sales executives are being asked to do more with less. It's a demand many have heard in previous hard times, and most managers muddled through then. But the nature of the current downturn—and of the changes the marketing and sales environment has undergone since the 2001–02 recession—suggests that those who follow the survival techniques of past slowdowns risk betting on the wrong markets, customers, advertising vehicles, or sales approaches.

In previous downturns, many marketers doubled down on large, historically profitable customers, geographies, and market segments. Today, this approach may prove ineffective because the world's economic woes are affecting customers and markets in unexpected and extremely specific ways. Marketers should therefore toss out those historical expectations and focus on the emerging pockets of customer profitability.

Cash-strapped marketers have also typically emphasized traditional media, such as television and newspaper ads, while cutting back on new advertising vehicles. But marketing has evolved rapidly over the past decade, with traditional media declining in importance as the Internet and social networking achieved meaningful scale. Marketing executives trying to rationalize media spending must factor this new balance into their austerity programs.

Another common approach for marketers trying both to cut costs and safeguard revenue has been to slash back-office sales overhead while continuing to invest in frontline salespeople. The evolution of the sales force in recent years means that marketers should take a much more nuanced approach. Companies used to regard the "feet on the street" model as their primary lever for increasing sales. Now they rely on a mixed model—customer-centric frontline product specialists and industry-specific sales managers who play a coordinating role—to provide better service and target new revenue opportunities.[1] If executives ignore these new practices when they rationalize sales programs, hard-won customer relationships, revenue streams, and margin gains may be at risk.

Of course, not everything from the past is outmoded: marketers must still reexamine the value propositions of their brands, fine-tune products and pricing, and manage the cost of media agencies and other vendors carefully. But these steps aren't enough. To weather the storm, it will be necessary to identify anew who and where the profitable customers are and to prioritize the most effective marketing and sales vehicles for reaching them.

When marketing and sales executives do so, it's critical to bear something in mind: the broader forces at work in the global economy mean that the underlying economics of strategies could continue shifting with unprecedented speed and scale. Such extreme uncertainty demands constant attention, frequent reprioritization, and strategies that anticipate and respond to a changing landscape.

Where to invest sales and marketing resources
The impact of recessions always varies across economies; for one thing, unemployment levels rise at different rates in different regions. This time around, however, global economic conditions are affecting different geographies and demographic groups in even more diverse and complex ways.

- A global credit crunch and the attendant volatility in commodities are whipsawing economies around the world in different ways at different times, which means the relative attractions and risks of customers and countries are shifting rapidly.

- The housing sector is contracting in markets around the world, but the level of mortgage default rates and the effect on consumer spending vary across and within regions. In the United States, for example, Arizona, California, Florida, Michigan, and Nevada have been hard hit, other states less so.

[1] For more on collaborative selling, see Maryanne Q. Hancock, Roland H. John, and Philip J. Wojcik, "Better B2B selling," mckinseyquarterly.com, June 2005.

• Historically attractive demographic groups have experienced major reversals of fortune. The nest eggs and retirement prospects of the baby boomers, for example, have been dramatically reduced by rapid declines in equity and housing values. This development raises the possibility of significant shifts in spending.

These disruptions suggest that the old tactic of focusing on historically profitable regions and customer groups will miss the mark. Instead, marketing and sales executives must reprioritize geographic markets and customer segments at every shift of economic fortune.

Reprioritizing geographies

Multinational companies will have to reassess their growth forecasts for the countries where they compete. Even assessments conducted as recently as 2008 should be reexamined, since the crisis has affected every country on Earth.

One global technology company, for example, recently began a major repositioning that shifted its marketing expenditures from developed countries to emerging ones offering higher projected growth rates and weaker competitive pressures. Recent economic events, though, have invalidated some of the territory-by-territory profit assumptions and significantly changed the time horizons of expected growth for others. The company recognized that its broad-based pre-crisis repositioning effort would generate disappointing results, so it is now working to identify markets with better prospects in this tough economic environment.

Companies can protect their revenues and profit margins by taking this granular approach a step further. Even within sectors or geographies that seem down across the board, the rates at which potential customers grow or decline vary substantially. While it is well known that the US manufacturing sector, for example, has weakened considerably over the past few years, manufacturing GDP has actually expanded in many counties across the country. In fact, from 2006 to 2007 the manufacturing revenues of companies in these counties rose by $97 billion,[2] roughly two-thirds of China's manufacturing growth over the same period. In Michigan, one of the hardest-hit states in the US Midwest, growth rates vary by double-digit percentages, and manufacturing revenues in the top counties rose by nearly $2 billion in 2007. Of course, no marketing strategy could now rely on these outdated figures. But a similar analysis today, probably at an even more detailed level, would in all likelihood help a company that sells manufacturing supplies to focus its scarce sales resources on

---

[2] Measured in 2000 US dollars.

growth counties instead of deploying resources across the board in a declining market.

Consumer marketers with access to micromarket data have even more opportunities to enhance profitability. One beverage company recently conducted surveys that identified staggering differences in the potential profitability of customers within individual markets and micromarkets. The price sensitivity of the respondents varied by as much as a factor of 13 across regional markets, a factor of 5 across cities within them, and a factor of 3 across zip codes within individual cities (Exhibit 1). Armed with this level of detail, a company can maximize its profitability by focusing on micromarkets less sensitive to prices while also offering discounts or preferential pricing elsewhere to drive sales volumes.

Reprioritizing consumer segments

Much as the profitability of different regions and micromarkets has shifted, fluctuating unemployment rates, equity prices, and housing and fuel costs have changed the profitability of consumer groups that cut

EXHIBIT 1

Looking at micromarkets

One company's markets and micromarkets, % of surveyed customers who said that price was 1 factor leading them to make fewer purchases (disguised company)

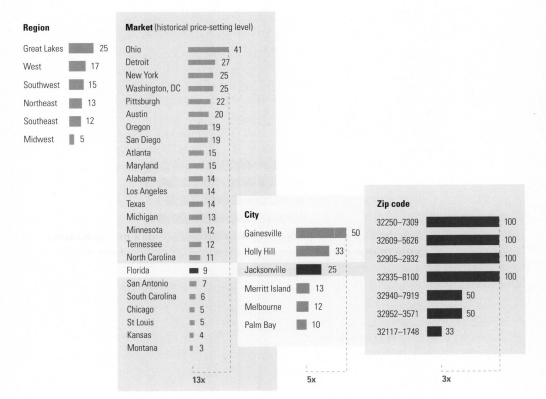

Region	
Great Lakes	25
West	17
Southwest	15
Northeast	13
Southeast	12
Midwest	5

Market (historical price-setting level)

Market	
Ohio	41
Detroit	27
New York	25
Washington, DC	25
Pittsburgh	22
Austin	20
Oregon	19
San Diego	19
Atlanta	15
Maryland	15
Alabama	14
Los Angeles	14
Texas	14
Michigan	13
Minnesota	12
Tennessee	12
North Carolina	11
Florida	9
San Antonio	7
South Carolina	6
Chicago	5
St Louis	5
Kansas	4
Montana	3

City

City	
Gainesville	50
Holly Hill	33
Jacksonville	25
Merritt Island	13
Melbourne	12
Palm Bay	10

Zip code

Zip code	
32250–7309	100
32609–5626	100
32905–2932	100
32935–8100	100
32940–7919	50
32952–3571	50
32117–1748	33

13x   5x   3x

across geographies. In many cases, changes in consumer behavior will force companies to reallocate marketing resources from historically attractive segments. Some groups that until recently had been major contributors to spending growth will become less profitable. Affluent young professionals, many of whom work in the financial-services sector, probably won't continue to fuel historic levels of growth in luxury goods, for example.

In other cases, the shock of the economic crisis could accelerate longer-term shifts in the spending and attractiveness of segments, such as the baby boom generation in the United States, as well as its counterparts in Japan and Western Europe. The high spending rates of the boomers made them a sought-after and profitable customer segment for many companies. The "wealth effect" of real-estate appreciation, along with the gains (or hopes of future gains) of the equities in the boomers' retirement accounts, enabled much of this spending. Indeed, many boomers were borrowing against these assets to pay for their lifestyles.[3] As a result, US boomers have saved less for retirement than previous generations did.

Today, the one-two punch of depressed housing values and big losses in equities means that many boomers face uncertain retirement prospects and can't continue to spend as they once did. In fact, they will have to

[3]See David Court, Diana Farrell, and John E. Forsyth, "Serving aging baby boomers," mckinseyquarterly.com, November 2007; and Eric D. Beinhocker, Diana Farrell, and Ezra Greenberg, "Why baby boomers will need to work longer," in this issue.

E X H I B I T   2

Shifting priorities

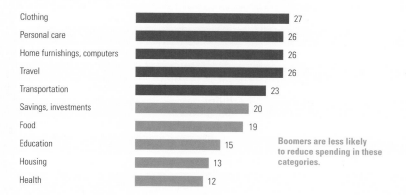

Categories boomers would cut when asked to reduce spending by 20%, % of boomers who elected given catagory

Clothing	27
Personal care	26
Home furnishings, computers	26
Travel	26
Transportation	23
Savings, investments	20
Food	19
Education	15
Housing	13
Health	12

Boomers are less likely to reduce spending in these categories.

Source: 2006 McKinsey survey of aging US consumers; McKinsey analysis

EXHIBIT 3

The morning after

Pocket margin[1] for leading manufacturer of industrial controls, top 7 accounts (disguised example), %

■ Q3 2007
■ Q3 2008

Company accounts

A 10.5 / 8.7
B 9.3 / 9.4
C 9.1 / 5.1
D 8.4 / 8.2
E 8.3 / 8.4
F 8.1 / 2.9
G 8.1 / 8.1

Changes in freight costs, product mixes, and payment behavior generate major shifts in profitability of an account.

One of the company's formerly more profitable accounts is now one of the least profitable.

[1] Pocket margin is a precise and comprehensive measure of customer profitability that includes all on- and off-invoice discounts and all account-specific costs to serve (eg, special handling and packaging, tech support).

reprioritize their spending across categories en masse. In 2006, when we asked boomers how they would cut their overall expenditures by 20 percent, the respondents singled out clothing, personal care, home furnishings, and travel for cuts but said they were less likely to reduce spending on necessities like food, housing, and health (Exhibit 2). For companies in the sectors, such as home furnishings, that will probably bear the brunt of these spending shifts, the task ahead is to target demographic segments with better growth prospects.

Reprioritizing business-to-business opportunities

Business-to-business (B2B) companies must go a step further. A fresh look at segments isn't enough; instead, such companies must reexamine their opportunities and risks on a customer-by-customer basis. Of course, they must start by assessing the basics: whether a customer has enough cash or liquidity and the likelihood that such funds will survive. Then they should think about how the crisis will affect all aspects of their profitability.

Many suppliers, for example, have long-standing agreements to offer volume-based rebates to their customers who are distributors. But the weak economy may cut the volumes of some distributors drastically, so that they no longer qualify. Similarly, some customers may find their economics undermined by volatility in the price of their key inputs, such as fuel and other commodities, and will therefore no longer be able to buy at the volumes and prices suppliers expect. Suppliers must stay alert to these possibilities and respond accordingly.

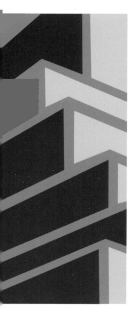

For a leading manufacturer of industrial controls, such shifts have drastically affected margins, transforming what a year ago was one of its most profitable accounts into one of the least profitable today (Exhibit 3). In the past, this account rated preferential attention and service, flexible terms, and high levels of tech support. Now, it calls for aggressive corrective action—reining in costs to serve, renegotiating rebates, encouraging more efficient order quantities—of a kind that would have been unthinkable not long ago.

How to invest marketing and sales resources
In addition to putting resources into the geographies and customers with the greatest profit potential, executives must emphasize the media and sales efforts most likely to deliver such profit. In previous downturns, that meant investing in proven advertising vehicles while cutting back on newer ones with shorter track records, as well as focusing resources on sales reps while trimming central back-office functions.

Over the past several years, however, the challenges of marketing proliferation have created a more complex mix of marketing vehicles and sales models.[4] Historical responses or across-the-board cuts may be exactly the wrong thing in this recession. A more nuanced approach is required.

Reprioritizing advertising vehicles
New communications vehicles such as the Internet, social networking, and mobile devices are gaining scale and delivering effective results. Meanwhile, classic media such as television have become, at a minimum, much more costly. Most marketing plans therefore try to meet their objectives cost-effectively by using a mix of traditional and new vehicles, with the latter typically accounting for 10 to 15 percent of spending.

A reprioritization of this kind requires a better understanding of the effectiveness of different forms of advertising than many marketers have today. These marketers, who assume the reach and cost of a vehicle serve as a proxy for its effectiveness, ignore the vehicle's quality—that is, its ability to influence customers. Quality is easiest to measure in direct businesses, which can precisely determine the return on investments in outbound catalogs or e-mails. But there are ways to estimate the quality even of harder-to-measure vehicles—such as television, product placements, and sponsorships—and to prioritize them accordingly.

Companies can maximize the accuracy of their quality assessments by combining a variety of information sources, such as quantitative

[4]For more on marketing proliferation, see David Court, Thomas D. French, and Trond Riiber Knudsen, "Profiting from proliferation," mckinseyquarterly.com, June 2006.

customer surveys, postevent focus groups (for sponsorships or other on-the-ground marketing efforts), and workshops where marketing managers and outside experts from advertising and media agencies piece together a collective point of view. Several major consumer companies that recently conducted such workshops found the consensus reached in them extremely consistent with more in-depth, quantitative studies.

No matter how a company arrives at its quality assessment, the real power comes from combining that analysis with data on the reach and cost of an advertising vehicle. This combination of reach, cost, and quality helps marketers compare the impact of different vehicles on an "apples to apples" basis—the key to effective prioritization. As the experience of one representative company demonstrates, it is not uncommon to find a hundredfold difference between the impact of two different vehicles (Exhibit 4). There is no consistent pattern indicating whether traditional or new vehicles have higher scores for reach, cost, or quality, so marketers must make their own objective comparisons to eliminate ineffective vehicles without hesitation and to support high-impact ones with confidence.

Reprioritizing sales functions

As we have seen, in tough times companies try to improve their profits by reducing sales overheads while concentrating resources on the frontline sales force. But today's sales teams use newer kinds of support that are too important to cut indiscriminately: they play strategic roles in the sales process and are critical to serving the most profitable customers and to converting new prospects. An executive who slashes these support functions as part of a broad cost-cutting campaign risks severely damaging the sales force's effectiveness.

Consider how recent changes have played out at a large industrial-services company. Ten years ago, 90 percent of its salespeople served either in account management or in the field. Only limited support was available, in the form of sales training, product information brochures, and a few product specialists. This company significantly increased the number of product specialists because its customers demanded greater expert assistance and its product range was expanding. It also added a pricing group for contract negotiations, industry-specific sales managers who provide additional expertise for customers, outbound telemarketing representatives who identify opportunities to gain small and midsize customers, and a customer and competitor analysis group to help decide how aggressively the company should support new opportunities.

In today's downturn, this organization's head of sales had to trim costs by 10 percent. Eliminating some product specialists, industry-oriented managers, and telemarketing support would probably cut the number

EXHIBIT 4

A range of effectiveness

Disguised example of company in men's personal-care market   ☐ Digital marketing vehicles

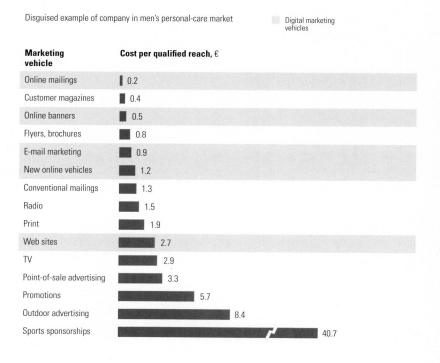

Marketing vehicle	Cost per qualified reach, €
Online mailings	0.2
Customer magazines	0.4
Online banners	0.5
Flyers, brochures	0.8
E-mail marketing	0.9
New online vehicles	1.2
Conventional mailings	1.3
Radio	1.5
Print	1.9
Web sites	2.7
TV	2.9
Point-of-sale advertising	3.3
Promotions	5.7
Outdoor advertising	8.4
Sports sponsorships	40.7

of new leads and win rates so much that sales would fall more than they would if the company eliminated an equal number of salespeople or account managers. Similarly, thinning out the pricing or competitor analysis teams might lead to poor pricing decisions that would depress margins or to the wasting of time on unrewarding sales prospects. An analysis of win rates and profit margins on new contracts helped the head of sales to confirm that the retention of product specialists and pricing specialists was crucial to maintaining profitability.

Instead of making across-the-board overhead cuts, a company can rationalize its sales programs while maintaining performance in a variety of ways. Assessing the current sales-coverage model helps the company determine which selling and sales-support formulas are most effective for which types of customers and sales situations and then to rebalance resources as needed. In practice, this approach might mean handling reorders online, covering basic sales and account-management tasks through telesales representatives, and using larger response teams to address major requests for proposals. Another important step is to analyze win–loss ratios in difficult customer negotiations with an eye to determining which sales support groups are most effective and which contribute less and can therefore be trimmed.

Streamlining the after-sales process and establishing the appropriate level of customer support can shrink costs as well. Critical to all these moves is an understanding of what customers expect and of the importance of after-sales support to their overall experience.

The author gratefully acknowledges the contributions of Thomas Baumgartner, Jonathan Gordon, Maryanne Hancock, Dieter Kiewell, Mike Marn, and Jesko Perrey.

A nuanced approach like this can help sales and marketing executives to identify cost savings more confidently and to protect the people and programs making a direct contribution to profitability.

We welcome your comments on this article. Please send them to quarterly_comments@ mckinsey.com.

Companies that follow the playbook from past recessions will probably chase markets and segments made less attractive by the present downturn and focus too many resources on traditional marketing vehicles and frontline salespeople. To avoid these costly mistakes, marketing and sales executives must dynamically reassess their geographic, customer, advertising, and sales force priorities, with constant attention to the ever-shifting economics of this downturn.

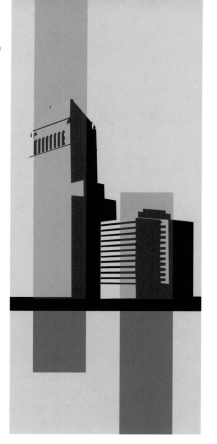

Why the crisis hasn't shaken the cost of capital

The long-term cost of capital hasn't increased so far in the downturn—and didn't in past recessions.

Richard Dobbs, Bin Jiang, and Timothy M. Koller

The cost of capital for companies reflects the attitudes of investors toward risk—specifically, the reward they expect for taking risks. If they become more averse to risk, companies have difficulty raising capital and may need to cancel or defer some investments or to forgo some mergers and acquisitions. So it's understandable that the current financial crisis has many executives concerned about what the price of risk—the cost of capital—will mean for their strategic decisions in the near term.

Yet our analysis finds no evidence that the long-term price of risk has increased over its historical levels—even though short-term capital is difficult to obtain. Anyone with a longer-term view won't find this surprising. At the peak of the tech bubble of 2000, when the media were awash with suggestions that the cost of capital had permanently declined, a deeper analysis suggested that it was remarkably stable— and has been for the past 40 years.[1]

Richard Dobbs is a director in McKinsey's Seoul office; **Bin Jiang** is a consultant in the New York office, where **Tim Koller** is a principal.

Obviously, for companies that are concerned about survival and having difficulty raising capital, its cost is clearly irrelevant. We realize some companies just don't have access to new capital, period. Yet

[1] See Marc H. Goedhart, Timothy M. Koller, and Zane D. Williams, "The real cost of equity," mckinseyquarterly.com, October 2002.

for companies that have more of it than they need to survive—either from internally generated funds or the long-term-debt markets—assumptions about its cost can make the difference between snapping up promising opportunities or being overtaken by competitors.

To understand changes in the weighted average cost of capital (WACC), we need to examine, in nominal terms, its component parts: the cost of equity and the cost of debt.

Cost of equity

We infer changes in the cost of equity by examining changes in equity values and in expected future profits and cash flows. Neither of these can be measured straightforwardly.

The S&P 500's climax—1,500, in 2007—reflected extraordinarily high profits in the financial, petroleum, and mining sectors and above-trend profits in many others.[2] To normalize the level of equity prices, we compared the long-term relationship between GDP growth and corporate profits. We estimated that, in mid-2008, the long-term sustainable level of corporate earnings would suggest a price level for the S&P 500 of about 1,100 to 1,200.[3] At the time of writing, the index was fluctuating in the 900-to-950 range, a decline of 15 to 25 percent from this sustainable level.

We can also calibrate this decline with the decline in share prices of those companies that did not experience the same earnings bubble and that have stable earnings, such as consumer staples. We find that these companies, which have had more stable earnings, are a stronger benchmark for assessing the economy-wide cost of capital. Their share prices at the time of this writing were down by about 15 to 20 percent from peak levels. Admittedly, this calculation isn't exact, and prices change daily.

The second factor in assessing the cost of equity capital is the ongoing level of corporate profits, which typically falls in recessions as GDP trend growth declines. History suggests that a recession involving a 5 to 10 percent decline in the cumulative long-term GDP trend would permanently reduce the corporate-profits trend line also by 5 to 10 percent.

Now let's pull these variables together into a discounted-cash-flow model. A midpoint estimate of the share-price decline—20 percent—and a 7.5 percent decline in the profit trend line translate into a hike in the cost of equity capital of about half of a percentage point. That

[2] See Marc H. Goedhart, Bin Jiang, and Timothy M. Koller, "Market fundamentals: 2000 versus 2007," mckinseyquarterly.com, September 2007.
[3] See Richard Dobbs, Bin Jiang, and Timothy M. Koller, "Preparing for a slump in earnings," mckinseyquarterly.com, March 2008.

is within the usual allowances for measurement error and within the range of annual market fluctuations.

Note that this analysis does not make allowance for the expected sharper short-term drop in corporate profits or for the market's tendency to overreact to recessions. Taking all these factors into account, we think there has been no significant change in the long-term cost of equity capital.

But this is based on our assumptions: Exhibit 1 allows you to construct your own estimate of the change in the cost of equity capital. For it to increase by a full percentage point, share prices would have to decline by 25 percent from their normal levels while profits remained relatively stable. Mathematically, a bigger drop in profits, which some expect, would mean an even smaller increase in the cost of capital.

Some might object that very few public offerings of equity have been floated recently. Our answer is that prices of liquid shares on stock exchanges are the best indicator of what investors will pay for shares. Others might counter that the economy faces extraordinarily high uncertainty right now. That is true, but uncertainty affects industries differently and therefore ought to be built into cash flow projections rather than the cost of equity. A single uncertainty risk premium should not apply to the entire economy.

Cost of long-term debt

The cost of debt is the second component of the cost of capital. It's easy to assume the cost of debt has increased, considering the increase

EXHIBIT 1

Minimal impact

Change in cost of equity, percentage point

Changes in earnings (each year in perpetuity), %

		−10.0	−7.5	−5.0	−2.5	0	
Changes in share prices,%	−25	0.8	0.9	1.1	1.2	1.3	Cost of equity increases by ≥1 percentage point.
	−20	0.5	0.6	0.7	0.9	1.0	
	−15	0.2	0.4	0.5	0.6	0.7	
	−10	0.0	0.1	0.2	0.3	0.4	20% reduction in share price combined with 7.5% profit decline = 0.6 percentage point increase in cost of equity capital.
	−5	−0.2	−0.1	0.0	0.1	0.2	
Cost of equity decreases	0	−0.4	−0.3	−0.2	−0.1	0	

EXHIBIT 2

A growing spread

10-year constant maturity bond yields for nonfinancial companies, %

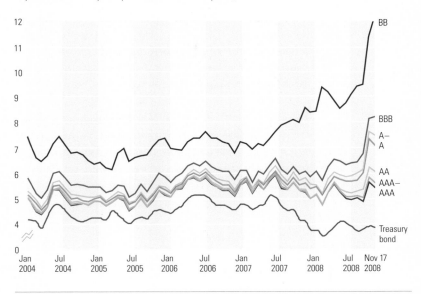

Source: Bloomberg

EXHIBIT 3

Cheaper debt?

Moody's average annual bond index yields for nonfinancial companies, %

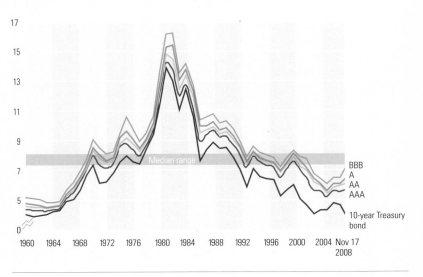

Source: Moody's; Bloomberg

in absolute rates on corporate bonds and the spread between Treasury and corporate bonds in recent months (Exhibit 2). As a benchmark, the yield to maturity on A-rated bonds rose a little more than one percentage point, to about 7 percent, from September to November 2008.

When you take a longer-term perspective, though, 7 percent isn't unusually high. Only during 6 of the past 20 years has the cost of debt for A-rated companies been lower than that (Exhibit 3).

In all likelihood, the spread is increasing as a result of high demand for Treasury bonds—a demand that depresses their yields—not because investment-grade corporate bonds are becoming more risky. The rates and spreads of the past several years were probably unsustainably low and current levels are simply a reversion to normality.

EXHIBIT 4

From a point of strength

Ratio of debt to EBITA[1] for nonfinancial S&P 500 companies

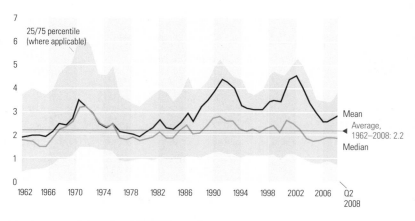

Interest coverage ratio for nonfinancial S&P 500 companies

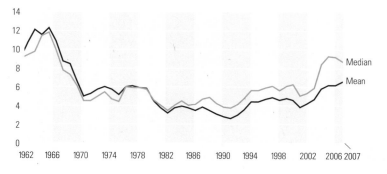

[1] Earnings before interest, taxes, and amortization.

The impact of the increasing cost of debt on a company's WACC is mitigated by the tax deductibility of debt and by the conservatism of the capital structures of most investment-grade companies, which means that the cost of debt is a smaller proportion of the WACC. Indeed, nonfinancial S&P 500 companies have less debt today than they have had for most of the past 40 years (Exhibit 4).

Implications

In sum, despite the decline in equity values and the increasing spreads on corporate debt, there is no evidence of a substantial increase in the cost of long-term capital. Of course, we cannot be certain that its cost will not increase over the next several years as the recession develops.

One unknown that demands caution is the outlook for inflation or deflation. The analysis above is on a nominal basis. For real cost of capital not to change, we need to assume that long-term inflation remains stable, at 2 to 3 percent. Some analysts are concerned about deflation, at least in the short term; others about inflation as governments around the world flood their economies with money. Deflation or high levels of inflation for an extended period could change investors' appetite for risk and the real cost of capital, along with other economic relationships.

We welcome your comments on this article. Please send them to quarterly_comments@ mckinsey.com.

Nonetheless, as with all valuations, the uncertainty of cash flows has a much bigger effect on value than changes in the cost of capital. That uncertainty has increased significantly. It is particularly unclear what a normal level of growth and returns on capital will be in the future. The credit bubble has distorted both during the past few years.

Innovation lessons from the 1930s

History suggests that even the deepest downturns can create huge opportunities for companies with money and ideas.

Tom Nicholas

Recent turmoil in global financial markets and its spillover into the real economy have generated considerable interest in the Great Depression. There's much to be fascinated with, both in the parallels (banking failures, a large spike in real-estate foreclosures, and global uncertainty, for example) and the points of contrast (such as the speed and coordination of the response of central banks and finance ministries in 2008).

Can the business practices of the 1930s yield useful lessons for executives setting priorities in today's uncertain and evolving environment? For investments to promote innovation, the answer may be yes. Executives are often told to maintain investment during downturns. It's easy to question this countercyclical advice, however, in times like the Depression or the present, when the volatility of financial markets (an indicator of uncertainty) reaches historic highs. Is the typical behavior of executives—act cautiously and delay investment projects until confidence returns—the wiser course?

Tom Nicholas is an associate professor at the Harvard Business School, where he teaches business history and entrepreneurial management.

Many companies hesitated to innovate during the 1930s. Consider, for example, patent applications as a proxy for resources devoted to innovation. The growth rate of US patent applications by companies with R&D laboratories was considerably lower during the 1930s than in the preceding decade. On the whole, corporate executives considering plans for research investments preferred to wait and see.

Furthermore, patent applications were far more synchronized with the business cycle during the Depression, when the cycle was extremely volatile, than they had been during the '20s, when economic conditions were buoyant (exhibit). From 1929 to 1937, for example, there were five years of GDP growth and four years of GDP contraction. Patent applications generally followed the same pattern, lagging behind by one year: the number of patent applications increased during years following GDP growth and decreased during years following GDP contraction, with two exceptions: 1934 and 1935. As the economy whipsawed companies during the 1930s, they appear to have regularly adjusted their views about the payoff from innovation.

Yet several successful companies did not delay such investments. One was DuPont. In April 1930, a noted DuPont research scientist, Wallace

EXHIBIT

Synchronized

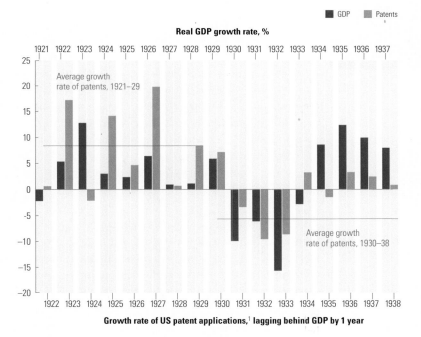

Real GDP growth rate, %

Growth rate of US patent applications,[1] lagging behind GDP by 1 year

[1] By companies with R&D laboratories.

Source: Malhar Nabar and Tom Nicholas, *Uncertainty and Innovation at the Time of the Great Depression*, Harvard Business School Working Paper, October 2008; patent application data from the European Patent Office's PATSTAT database matched against corporate research and development facilities as listed in editions of *Industrial Research and Development Laboratories of the United States* (National Research Council, 1921, 1927, 1931, 1933, 1938); GDP data from *Historical Statistics of the United States* (Cambridge University Press, 2006)

Carothers, recorded the initial discovery of neoprene (synthetic rubber). Although the company's price levels and sales fell by roughly 10 and 15 percent, respectively, that year, DuPont boosted R&D spending to develop the new technology commercially. A buyer's market for research scientists and low raw-material prices helped the company to keep the cost of its research investments manageable. Neoprene, which DuPont publicly announced in November 1931 and introduced commercially in 1937, became one of the 20th century's major innovations. By 1939, every automobile and airplane manufactured in the United States had neoprene components. Similarly, DuPont discovered nylon in 1934 and introduced it in 1938 after intensive R&D and product development.

DuPont isn't the only such example. Many new technology companies— for instance, Hewlett-Packard and Polaroid—that became leading innovators later in the century were established as entrepreneurial start-ups during the 1930s. Radio Corporation of America, the high-tech company whose stock was bludgeoned during the Great Crash, returned to profitability in 1934 as it shifted its innovation efforts from radio to the nascent television market. In total, US companies founded at least 73 in-house R&D labs each year from 1929 to 1936.

Of course, these examples don't mean that aggressive investments for innovation would have been wise for every company during the 1930s or are universally wise today. But taken together, the patent research and the experience of successful innovators in those years suggest that although delay is the natural response to uncertainty, some companies should continue innovating even in an extraordinarily deep economic downturn—especially with technologies that take a long time to commercialize after discovery. Companies that delay these investments may forego significant growth opportunities when uncertainty subsides and the economy recovers.

We welcome your
comments on this article.
Please send them to
quarterly_comments@
mckinsey.com.

The experience of the 1930s also illustrates a broader point. Although deep downturns are destructive, they can also have an upside. The Depression-era economist Joseph Schumpeter emphasized the positive consequences of downturns: the destruction of underperforming companies, the release of capital from dying sectors to new industries, and the movement of high-quality, skilled workers toward stronger employers. For companies with cash and ideas, history shows that downturns can provide enormous strategic opportunities. ▼

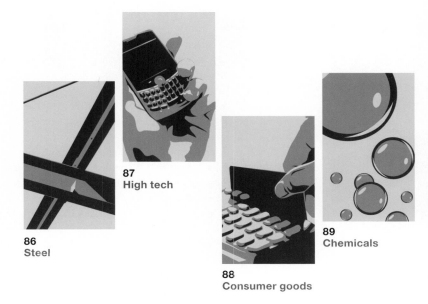

87
High tech

86
Steel

89
Chemicals

88
Consumer goods

Industry trends in the downturn:
A snapshot

In times of great uncertainty, an understanding of long-term industry trends can help executives plot robust strategies. This roundup highlights structural issues likely to influence the future performance of four industries: steel, technology, consumer goods, and chemicals.

Steel

As credit markets capsized in the third quarter of 2008, construction projects slowed and consumer spending decreased, stalling growth in the steel industry. Nonetheless, our research indicates that the long-term strength of global steel intensity (the amount of steel needed per dollar of global GDP) will probably fuel growing demand for many years to come, to as much as two billion tons annually by 2025.

As recently as the 1990s, the maturing of markets in Europe and North America reduced the level of steel intensity as the demand curve for automobiles, refrigerators, and infrastructure leveled off. Since the turn of the decade, infrastructure and construction projects linked to urbanization—mostly in China but also in India, the Middle East, and other regions—have accounted for more than 35 percent of global steel demand and for more than half

its growth. Demand for other metals, such as aluminum and copper, also exceeds GDP growth in these regions.

While their continuing development should support the industry over the long term, the immediate impact of the credit crunch will in all likelihood be reduced demand for steel—not only because end-user demand will diminish, but also because players along the supply chain will probably use up existing stocks. In addition, the crunch will inhibit short-term expansion plans for new steel-making and -mining capacity around the world, and that is likely to create a more volatile balance between demand and supply. Within a few years, however, expansion may resume as the industry works to keep up with growing demand in emerging markets.

Frank Bekaert is a principal in McKinsey's Luxembourg office, and **Benedikt Zeumer** is a principal in the Düsseldorf office.

Steel intensity (global consumption volumes relative to global GDP[1]); index: steel intensity in 1992 = 100

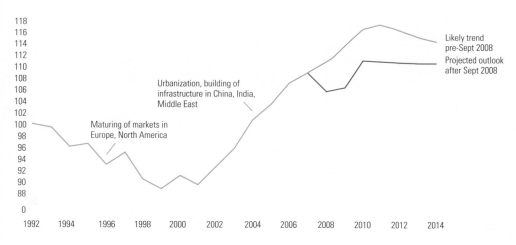

[1] Adjusted for purchasing-power parity.

High Tech

During recessions, tech spending has historically fallen more than GDP has. Our research (covering economic downturns in 50 countries over the past 13 years) indicates that IT spending typically fell 5 to 7 times further than GDP, with the most severe declines in hardware (which fell 8 to 9 times GDP) and less severe ones in software and services (3 to 5 times GDP).

The decline was much larger during the 2001 downturn because spending on computing and telecommunications equipment as a percentage of GDP (IT intensity) had previously soared to historic levels. A boom in tech start-ups, along with Y2K fears, promoted a spending surge on communications equipment, servers, and a range of other products. When the economic slowdown arrived, start-ups foundered, many companies had too much tech and telecom capacity, and spending cuts across

the economy were severe. Chastened by that experience, many companies have since pressured their CIOs to manage IT more effectively.

As the economy enters the current slowdown, the growth of IT intensity is closer to its historic trend—even slightly below the ten-year average. While most companies are reviewing their IT budgets in an effort to reduce overall spending, many are trying to maintain high-priority investments. The uncertainty of today's business environment makes it perilous to predict technology spending, but it does seem likely that the sector's experience could be more in line with historic trends than it was in 2001.

Eric Kutcher is a principal in McKinsey's Stamford office, and Dilip Wagle is a principal in the Seattle office.

IT intensity (% of GDP spent on IT)

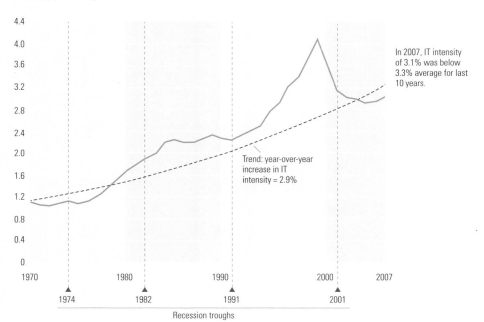

In 2007, IT intensity of 3.1% was below 3.3% average for last 10 years.

Trend: year-over-year increase in IT intensity = 2.9%

Recession troughs

Consumer goods

Betsy Bohlen and **Kristi Weaver** are consultants in McKinsey's Chicago office.

Recessions have affected spending on different categories of consumer goods in different ways. An analysis of consumer spending during the 1990–91 and 2001–02 downturns shows that US consumers changed their priorities instead of making across-the-board cuts. Daily amenities—eating out, personal-care products and services, and apparel—tended to suffer. But categories such as groceries and reading materials, which substituted for more expensive options, actually benefitted from higher spending, as did less discretionary items, like insurance and health care. Spending on education showed the biggest increase. While these historical trends are instructive, they may not tell the whole story this time around: tighter consumer credit, low personal-savings rates, and declining home values may cause individuals to cut spending faster and further across more categories. Even so, some categories will weather the storm better than others. Companies that react to the downturn with an understanding of their categories' likely performance will have a better chance.

Average growth in US consumer expenditures for recession (1990–91 and 2001–02) compared with average growth for entire period (1984–2006); index: average growth for entire period = 0

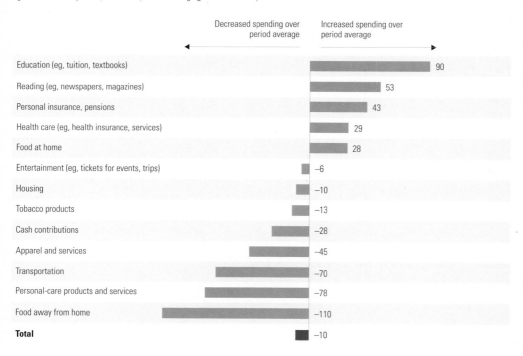

Chemicals

Global chemical production hasn't declined in a sustained way since the early 1980s. The result then was an industry restructuring, with lower-cost new plants replacing older, less efficient, and smaller-scale ones that had lower margins. Subsequent downturns have compressed margins, delayed expansion plans, and given players with strong balance sheets opportunities to acquire undervalued competitors. Those downturns did not, however, lead to a significant industry restructuring. A major downturn today could be different: depressed demand may help new low-cost capacity in China and the Middle East more quickly displace production in higher-cost operations in Europe, Japan, North America, and South Korea.

Scott Andre is a consultant in McKinsey's Houston office.

Annual change in petrochemical consumption by volume,[1] %

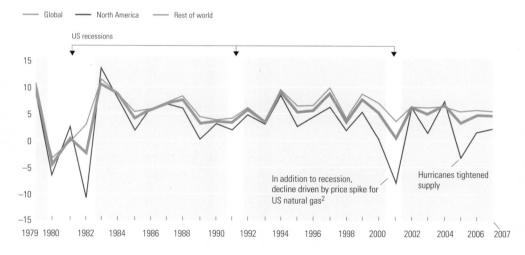

[1] Includes production of >90 petrochemicals; excludes a few major products—eg, ammonia, chlorine, methanol, urea.
[2] High natural-gas prices made production less competitive in United States than in other regions.

Source: Tecnon; US Bureau of Economics Analysis

Managing regulation in a new era

As concern over global problems mounts, executives and regulators have everything to gain from building relationships based on trust, and developing solutions that benefit a wide range of stakeholders.

Scott C. Beardsley, Luis Enriquez, and Robin Nuttall

The 2008 financial crisis may come to be seen as the demarcation between two regulatory eras. For the past generation, free markets have enjoyed a remarkable intellectual and political ascendancy, championed by academics and governments alike as the best way to promote continuing growth and stability. Now the world suddenly appears to think that some problems are too big and threatening to be solved by free-wheeling businesses. Politicians and commentators of every stripe are calling for greater regulation.

Like most big shifts in the intellectual and political climate, this one appears at first glance to have burst forth overnight. In fact, it's been bubbling beneath the surface far longer. There has been a gradual awareness that self-regulation and corporate social responsibility go only so far in solving big problems. On the day in September 2008 when Lehman Brothers collapsed and the financial crisis became a financial calamity, you may have missed a less prominent news item. Ian Cheshire, CEO of the UK retailer Kingfisher, told the BBC that "there are certain things that are too big, too long-term . . . to deal with incrementally. We need a government framework." Cheshire, a member of the UK Corporate Leaders Group on Climate Change, was speaking in support of a European effort to reduce greenhouse gas emissions.

Scott Beardsley is a director in McKinsey's Brussels office, where **Luis Enriquez** is a principal; **Robin Nuttall** is a principal in the London office.

A comment by Peter Brabeck-Letmathe, Nestlé's chairman, also failed to attract much attention: "Even though we have perhaps more impact than any other food company, we can only be a small part of the solution [to food and water problems]. The fact is that all our efforts, and those of other companies and consumers, will be in vain if governments throughout the world continue with their short-sighted policies instead of working towards solutions." He too was calling for more state intervention, not unfettered free markets.

Today a pattern is emerging. Tight credit; looming energy, food, and water shortages; and greenhouse gas emissions are high on the minds of business leaders as well as politicians. Consumers too are increasingly worried—and aware that an interconnected global economy means interconnected global problems. They hear about ice caps melting and banks collapsing in distant countries and know that all this matters to their lives, their jobs, their homes, their families. What's more, they expect companies to help alleviate these problems.[1] Such developments underscore the expansion of the "social contract" between business and society. The contract includes not only laws and regulations but also a growing obligation for companies to fulfill certain social responsibilities.

From antagonism to cooperation

Against this background of changing perceptions and priorities, regulation is set to assume fresh importance. As always, regulators should find the right ways to mitigate broader market failures—for example, to protect consumers and control environmental pollution—while also seeking to facilitate fair and intense competition among companies, for that will encourage larger increases in productivity, a faster-growing economy, and greater wealth for society to share.[2]

How should companies prepare? In the previous era, the answer would have been to hire more lawyers and lobbyists and send them off to do battle with regulators. Robert Reich, President Bill Clinton's first secretary of labor, describes in his 2007 book, *Supercapitalism*, the way intense competition has driven US companies in particular to dramatically increase their efforts to contest every regulatory decision affecting their profitability. Regulation has developed from a legal and political system that is structurally adversarial, so it is no surprise that adversarial attitudes and skills have set the tone in regulatory affairs. But an arms race of investment in legal and lobbying capacity makes less and less sense if governments, policy makers, and companies are to find optimal solutions to huge economic and sociopolitical challenges.

[1] See Sheila M. J. Bonini, Greg Hintz, and Lenny T. Mendonca, "Addressing consumer concerns about climate change," mckinseyquarterly.com, March 2008.
[2] See Scott C. Beardsley and Diana Farrell, "Regulation that's good for competition," mckinseyquarterly.com, May 2005.

Our research shows that companies are beginning to recognize this truth. In a September 2008 *McKinsey Quarterly* survey of 1,500 executives,[3] the respondents saw regulators as the primary source of the political and social pressures facing companies around the world. But many of these executives were unsure how to respond. They saw lobbying as an overused tool. When we asked them which issues would gain companies little praise for getting things right and a lot of criticism for getting things wrong, "political engagement and influence" came second only to the top team's remuneration.

In practice, companies have three options when they seek to engage a regulator (exhibit). They can maintain arm's-length, often adversarial relationships—limiting communications, so far as possible, to answering requests and deploying legal instruments such as appeals and challenges. At the other extreme, they can seek to build collaborative partnerships with the regulator. Neither model is typically optimal from a company's point of view. The arm's-length approach makes it hard to achieve trade-offs with the regulator and therefore generates antagonism. The collaborative-partnership model is bound to fail, since the regulator is fundamentally a policeman, not a partner.

[3] See "From risk to opportunity—How global executives view sociopolitical issues: McKinsey Global Survey Results," mckinseyquarterly.com, October 2008.

EXHIBIT

Engaging the regulator

	Arm's length	**Constructive engagement**	**Collaborative partnership**
The regulator . . .	. . . protects consumers and promotes competition—but at the expense of industry efficiency and long-term sustainability.	. . . makes the industry function effectively and efficiently, balances multiple stakeholder interests, has a clear vision for the future of the industry.	. . . is a key partner in ensuring optimum industry outcomes.
Company lets the regulator see . . .	. . . the legal minimum.	. . . as much as it can, while maintaining a small "walled garden" to allow private internal company discussions.	. . . anything it wants to know. The company is open about problems with data.
The company communicates with the regulator . . .	. . . only through the regulatory department, in a limited and very controlled way.	. . . directly at senior levels across the organization—eg, quarterly board-to-board interactions.	. . . openly and informally at many levels of the organization, relying on the regulatory department as a source of expertise.
Conflict with the regulator . . .	. . . is frequent, public, and normal, including going to court.	. . . is something the company has processes in place to avoid if at all possible—especially going to court.	. . . is something the company goes out of its way to avoid—even to the extent of admitting fault preemptively.
Transparency with the regulator . . .	. . . is limited to responding to formal requests for information.	. . . involves proactively sharing models with it to establish common fact base.	. . . means the full, open-book approach.

A better approach—and not only in a time of economic crisis—is an open dialogue aiming for constructive engagement with the regulator. Disagreement between the two parties is inevitable. Still, companies have a lot to gain, both for strategic and tactical reasons, from building trust and fostering long-term cooperation not only on small industry issues but also on large ones that may have socio-political dimensions.

One argument for the cooperative approach is that regulation is a game played over and over. In many cases, a company persuades a regulator that now is not the time to allow more competition, require reduced emissions, impose higher service obligations, or whatever—only to do much better than the regulator expected in the ensuing regulatory period. Regulators usually react to attempts to fool them by imposing a much harsher settlement in the next round. Trust can fall so far that regulators and companies must communicate through third parties.

This is not the first time we have shared such insights from our work helping companies with their regulatory strategies.[4] What's new is this: global economic and sociopolitical challenges have become more acute, and the contract between business and society is expanding, which makes it more important than ever for executives in a wide range of sectors to think hard about their approach to regulatory issues. Companies and regulators don't always have to be adversaries—where there is trust, regulation can become a mechanism for industry-wide, even global, cooperation on issues ranging from financial prudence to scientific innovation and climate change. The negotiation of formal competitive rules in heavily regulated industries is not the whole of regulation.

Increasingly, we see that regulators and companies need to engage each other in an atmosphere characterized by fact-based analysis and trust: regulators can do so by understanding more fully the economics and long-term dynamics of the industries they oversee, and companies by looking for inherently sustainable solutions. Adversarial regulatory contests will no doubt continue, but executives are coming to realize that they must be flexible and ready to make trade-offs.

Network-based industries, such as telecommunications, power, and railroads, are a case in point. New infrastructure investments with very long payback periods (say, fiber networks for telecom services) won't be made unless operators are convinced they will yield satisfactory returns over a reasonable period of time. Regulators face a challenge in balancing the need for these investments with the

[4]See Scott C. Beardsley, Denis Bugrov, and Luis Enriquez, "The role of regulation in strategy," mckinseyquarterly.com, November 2005.

imperative to reduce end-user prices by encouraging competition and opening up the infrastructure to all players. Rather than bargain hard in order to deny or delay access to competitors across a whole network, some incumbents make a nuanced and well-informed case that takes the interests of governments and consumers into account. This approach might, for example, involve accepting the principle of open access—where competitors are already present— while keeping access temporarily closed in less developed areas, so that investment will flow into them. Although such a compromise won't maximize an incumbent's short-term profits, it might include reasonably favorable terms that wouldn't be subject to constant change.

Building transparency and trust

Understanding regulatory issues in extreme detail is a prerequisite not only for anticipating risks and opportunities but also for building mutually beneficial relationships, based on trust and transparency, with regulators.

Regulatory issues are often extremely complex and interdependent. The process is no less complicated, commonly involving overlapping reviews by a number of agencies. Minor tariff revisions can have a major impact on corporate profits. Structural policy changes can reshape a whole industry. Executives will always be behind the curve unless they diagnose each issue in the current and long-term landscape of regulation and understand the economic, social, and strategic impact of different regulatory outcomes. Without such an understanding, companies often respond in an ineffective and desultory way to the opportunities and risks.

Consider, as a cautionary tale, the regulation of fees for cross-border payments after the euro's introduction, in 2002. It was no secret that the European Commission was eager to demonstrate the benefits of a single currency. Yet banks in the eurozone failed to anticipate, and therefore to influence, a new rule specifying that they could charge no more for cross-border transactions than for national ones. In many markets, national payments had been provided without fees, while cross-border transactions carried charges to cover the extra expense. Banks therefore ended up with costs they couldn't recoup from customers.

Typically, the quest for a detailed understanding should start with an exercise to shed light on the main regulatory issues that could affect a business, both today and within 3 to 5 years—and sometimes even within 10 to 20 years. The exercise should also examine the level of uncertainty for each issue, the positions of the major stake-holders (such as competitors, consumers, employees, unions, government agencies, and environmental groups), and the value at stake and other implications for the stakeholders as well as the company itself. These implications could involve, for instance, investment decisions, price and service levels, productivity, tax revenues, and employment levels. Potential disruptions, such as new technologies that might change the regulatory game, should be examined as well. In considering alternative regulations, there is no substitute for fact-based analysis to determine the trade-offs that will inevitably have to be made. The devil is in the details: seemingly minor ones can be worth billions and make all the difference between success and failure.

The key to a productive relationship between companies and regulators is a full understanding of the other side's perspectives and objectives—an understanding that makes it possible to craft solutions meeting the needs of both parties. In such relationships, companies and regulators might not show all of their cards, but they would discuss short- and long-term issues and share important, detailed information. An atmosphere of trust and transparency is critical for crafting balanced and sustainable regulations, since companies usually understand the economic challenges better than regulators do. A business, for example, has the best feel for how quickly (and to what extent) it can redesign products to reduce carbon emissions and is better placed to estimate how quickly new technologies can be rolled out to customers.

Transparency's virtues were evident when a regulator challenged a public utility to justify its decision to include the costs of its corporate parent in the profit-and-loss account. This company not only responded with a detailed and open explanation of its underlying assumptions and numbers but also signaled a willingness to consider alternative accounting approaches. The regulator accepted the arguments and did not change the company's tariffs.

An open, long-term relationship with regulators also gives companies a chance to shape regulation. While some auto manufacturers have lobbied governments to slow down carbon emission standards, for example, others are developing the technology to meet them. By informally discussing the progress of such efforts with the regulator, these front-runners can influence its expectations of how much of a reduction technical innovation can achieve. Such companies stand to gain the most in the heavily regulated markets of the future.

Going for win–win solutions

To shape regulation, companies will have to make it a core element of their strategies and move regulatory affairs from the exclusive domain of legal, technical, and public-relations experts to the agenda of the CEO and the top team. The leaders of every business should develop a vision of its industry's future—a vision incorporating socio-political issues, incremental changes in the industry, and structural changes, such as technological discontinuities—and build the organizational capability to support and shape it. The statements by

Kingfisher's CEO and Nestlé's chairman reflect that kind of strategic, long-term approach to big sociopolitical issues and the resulting pressures for regulation.

A long-term view is critical when companies confront many forces poised to reshape their industries. Regulatory decisions often create more value to be shared—bigger cakes, not just bigger slices—but sometimes only if an industry's leading players allow this to happen. The introduction of the GSM[5] standard for mobile telephony in Europe, for example, was accomplished through a joint effort of governments, regulators, and companies. GSM opened up an enormous market, with benefits for companies, governments, and consumers alike: mobile-telephony revenues rose sharply, governments presided over rising national productivity and tax revenues, and customers got ever-lower prices and wider coverage. New services flourished. Many younger Europeans can hardly conceive of a world without text messages. In other parts of the world, the fragmentation of mobile standards held back growth for years.

The wisdom of looking for solutions that benefit such a wide range of stakeholders—especially consumers—is often apparent even when an individual company faces regulatory decisions. To succeed, its executives must understand the competing agendas of important stakeholders and work with them to build coalitions that translate corporate priorities into feasible compromises and sustainable outcomes.

Engaging stakeholders in this way can also be an investment in a company's reputation, and such investments are useful in dealing with customers and in future negotiations with regulators. Unilever, for example, decided to work directly with a prominent nongovernmental organization (NGO) to analyze in detail the impact on poverty of all the company's operations in a developing country. As part of this collaboration, Unilever granted the NGO unprecedented access to information and staff. The NGO came away from the project with a more positive view of this multinational corporation. Meanwhile, Unilever learned a great deal about how it could most cost-effectively have a positive influence in this country, in ways it hadn't previously considered. In addition, the company improved its reputation with the local authorities—an improvement that will undoubtedly serve it well in future negotiations with them—and showed customers that its commitment to alleviating poverty was more than PR.

In contrast, companies that take a short-term view, neglecting to base their positions on what might be sustainable in the eyes of regulators and other stakeholders, sometimes find themselves winning the battle but losing the war. Voluntary emission targets, for example, may help a business respond to environmental pressures on its own terms,

[5]Global System for Mobile communications, the global standard for mobile phones.

but to gain traction these targets must be credible. Motor manufacturers in the European Union didn't heed that reality when they embraced voluntary standards later deemed insufficient by regulators, which imposed far more demanding ones.

The regulatory challenge

Regulation is about solving problems that society or businesses can't solve alone, as well as making trade-offs among different objectives and the interests of various stakeholders.

These tasks will not become any easier. Regulators face, among other challenges, the need to take fast-moving sociopolitical dynamics into account when they address issues that have no clear "right" answer. Consider energy: at a time when many fear that control of fossil fuels will be used for political purposes and many countries are pushing to cut their carbon emissions, policy makers must decide whether to facilitate or to go on blocking the expansion of climate-friendly but controversial nuclear and large-scale hydro power.

As the world looks for regulations that can address these acute social challenges (and seize opportunities linked to them), policy makers and businesses must have an open dialogue about what would constitute success. Many objectives are conflicting in nature—such as attracting large investments to reduce greenhouse gas emissions while maintaining the lowest possible electricity prices—and it is essential for the regulatory process to ascertain the facts. Such a dialogue won't necessarily come up with an abstractly right answer but will help illuminate the trade-offs among various alternatives.

Leaders must also consider the proper level for regulations. Many problems can best be solved by individual countries or even localities. Nonetheless, a growing number of worldwide sociopolitical challenges—carbon emissions, the future of the banking system and capital markets, and technology standards, to name but a few—require regulatory standards at a transnational level. Solving the very complex issues involved in creating them calls for a give-and-take dialogue among politicians, regulators, business leaders, and other stakeholders.

The authors wish to acknowledge the contributions of their colleagues Norman Marshall and Sergio Sandoval.

In the coming new era of regulation, executives and regulators need, more than ever, to learn from each other. Only then will leaders succeed in crafting practical resolutions to sociopolitical issues and burning industry problems, such as those created by the financial crisis. In short, companies should take a strategic view of regulation and strive for solutions that benefit a wide range of stakeholders.▼

Strategy | **By Invitation:** Insights and opinion from outside contributors

Financial crisis and reform:

Looking back for clues to the future

Changes reaching far beyond the financial sector
have followed every major US financial crisis that
sparked an economic downturn.

Robert E. Wright

For the many global companies affected by the US business climate, an
obvious question in the wake of the financial system's recent upheaval
is the likelihood and extent of impending changes in the country's regulatory, political, and structural environment. History provides three
clear lessons: first, reforms followed every major US financial crisis that
led to an economic downturn. Second, the length and severity of the
postcrisis recession have historically been approximately proportional
to the degree of change that follows the recession. Finally, the resulting shifts commonly extend well beyond the financial-services sector.

Mild recessions, like those of 1990–91 and 2001, have typically led
to piecemeal regulatory reform (exhibit). Steeper downturns portended
seismic changes, such as major political realignments and even revolution. (Scholars are just now recognizing the important role that the
real estate bust of 1764–68—when land prices fell by half to two-
thirds in about a year and thousands of Americans ended up in debtors'
prison—played in the imperial crisis culminating in the events of
July 1776.) Similarly, the Panic of 1857 in the United States and the subsequent recession helped bring on the Civil War by exacerbating
sectional tensions over slavery and states' rights and helping the modern

Robert Wright is
a clinical associate
professor of economics
at New York University's
Stern School of
Business, where he
teaches business,
economic, and financial
history.

For another look on how past financial
crises affected the real economy,
read "Financial crises, past and present,"
on mckinseyquarterly.com.

Republican Party to coalesce. During the Great Depression, some
historians believe, the federal government averted rebellion thanks only
to the extraordinary changes ushered in by the first New Deal.

Nothing comparably dramatic seems imminent, but this doesn't mean
that game-changing regulatory reforms are impossible. Already, the
subprime-mortgage and liquidity crises have vastly increased the power
of the Federal Reserve System, the Federal Deposit Insurance
Corporation (FDIC), and the Treasury Department. While it's difficult
to predict what other shifts will transpire, the breadth of change
that has historically resulted from financial crises is worth bearing in
mind. The Panic of 1873 and the subsequent long recession, for
example, helped spur labor and agrarian unrest. Similarly, the recession
of 1893–97 invigorated Populism and Progressivism and paved the
way for the turn-of-century Great Merger Movement, which created
giant corporations such as U.S. Steel and International Harvester.
The Great Depression gave rise to the Glass–Steagall Act (which sepa-
rated investment and commercial banking for more than 60 years),
the FDIC, the Securities and Exchange Commission, and Social Security.

EXHIBIT

Times of crises

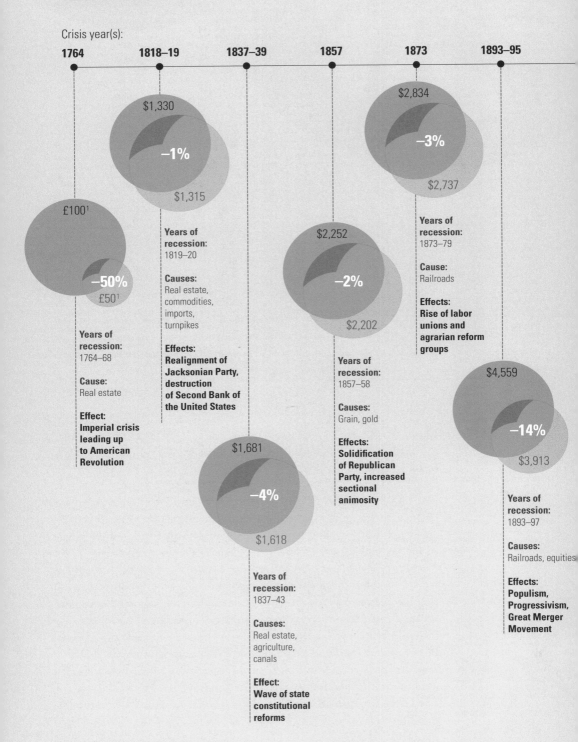

Crisis year(s):

| 1764 | 1818–19 | 1837–39 | 1857 | 1873 | 1893–95 |

$1,330
−1%
$1,315

$2,834
−3%
$2,737

£100[1]
−50%
£50[1]

Years of recession:
1764–68

Cause:
Real estate

Effect:
Imperial crisis leading up to American Revolution

Years of recession:
1819–20

Causes:
Real estate, commodities, imports, turnpikes

Effects:
Realignment of Jacksonian Party, destruction of Second Bank of the United States

$2,252
−2%
$2,202

Years of recession:
1873–79

Cause:
Railroads

Effects:
Rise of labor unions and agrarian reform groups

$4,559
−14%
$3,913

Years of recession:
1857–58

Causes:
Grain, gold

Effects:
Solidification of Republican Party, increased sectional animosity

$1,681
−4%
$1,618

Years of recession:
1893–97

Causes:
Railroads, equities

Effects:
Populism, Progressivism, Great Merger Movement

Years of recession:
1837–43

Causes:
Real estate, agriculture, canals

Effect:
Wave of state constitutional reforms

[1] Real estate prices.

Source: Land prices for troubled 1760s from numerous letters penned by Benjamin Franklin, other colonists; real per capita GDP statistics to 1790 from Measuring Worth; post-1857 recession dates from National Bureau of Economic Research

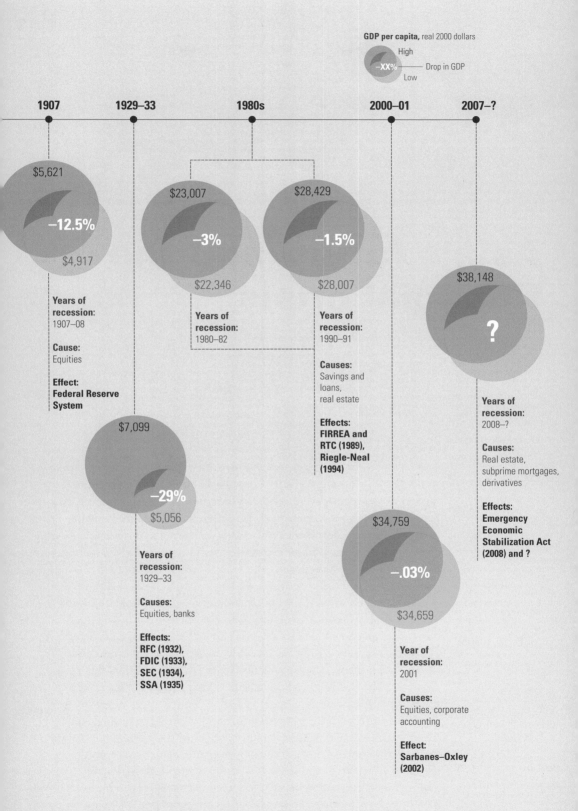

GDP per capita, real 2000 dollars

High
−XX% — Drop in GDP
Low

1907

$5,621

−12.5%

$4,917

Years of recession:
1907–08

Cause:
Equities

Effect:
Federal Reserve System

1929–33

$7,099

−29%

$5,056

Years of recession:
1929–33

Causes:
Equities, banks

Effects:
RFC (1932),
FDIC (1933),
SEC (1934),
SSA (1935)

1980s

$23,007

−3%

$22,346

Years of recession:
1980–82

$28,429

−1.5%

$28,007

Years of recession:
1990–91

Causes:
Savings and loans,
real estate

Effects:
FIRREA and RTC (1989),
Riegle-Neal (1994)

2000–01

$34,759

−.03%

$34,659

Year of recession:
2001

Causes:
Equities, corporate accounting

Effect:
Sarbanes–Oxley (2002)

2007–?

$38,148

?

Years of recession:
2008–?

Causes:
Real estate,
subprime mortgages,
derivatives

Effects:
Emergency Economic Stabilization Act (2008) and ?

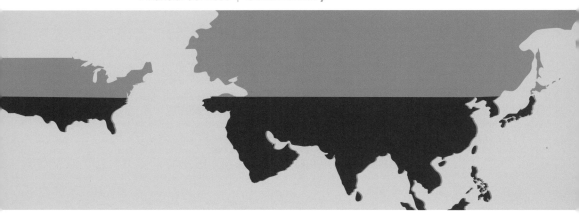

Asia's future and the financial crisis

The region has been hit hard but can help the world recover. Meanwhile, the global crisis is likely to spur further integration among Asian markets.

Dominic Barton

The collapse of Lehman Brothers triggered a global credit shock that struck with surprising force in Asia. Before Lehman's failure, many looked to the region as a bastion of economic stability. After all, Asia had high growth rates, large trade surpluses, and substantial foreign reserves. Its large companies were well capitalized and the books of its banks mostly free of the subprime loans and doubtful investments afflicting their Western peers.

Yet Asia couldn't avoid the economic fallout from the troubles of Europe and the United States: the region's stock markets plummeted, its currencies weakened, and its exports to the West slowed considerably. The impact of the crisis on the financial markets and real economies of Asia has largely ended speculation about its full "decoupling" from the West. The ties still bind. But the developments of the past few months reinforce our view that Asia should move more aggressively than ever to secure its economic future and improve its resilience in future crises. Asian governments must accelerate their plans to integrate regional economies—for instance, by boosting demand at home, speeding up intraregional trade and investment, and strengthening local and regional financial markets. Only through such initiatives can Asia hope to minimize the impact of future economic dislocations, whether they originate inside or outside the region.

Dominic Barton is a director in McKinsey's Shanghai office.

Asia's economies remain fundamentally sound. They will probably
emerge from the global downturn more rapidly than economies
in other regions will. Nonetheless, the crisis has exposed important
linkages between Asia, on the one hand, and Europe and the
United States, on the other. Asia depends heavily on external consumers: for example, in 2007, exports from Asian economies—
excluding Australia, Japan, and New Zealand—reached a high of
45 percent of regional GDP, up a full ten percentage points since
1995.[1] We estimate conservatively that Western consumers account
for about half of these exports, including both direct exports and
indirect exports through a growing intra-Asian reexport trade. Moreover, Western investors remain major players in most of Asia's
capital markets. Asian banks, except for those in China, are tightly
linked to Europe and the United States through the interbank market and US dollar liquidity needs.

Increased exports to the United States played an important role
in Asia's relatively swift recovery from the 1997–98 crisis and helped
China and India become economic giants. This time, however, US
consumers, with their troubled mortgages and maxed-out credit cards,
probably won't provide much relief. Asia's stock and bond markets
have deepened significantly since the last crisis: the value of equity and
debt markets in Asia, for instance, has soared to 140 percent of
regional GDP, up from 50 percent, in the past five years. But along with
this deepening has come significant foreign portfolio investment,
representing, for example, 30 to 40 percent of the money invested in
the financial markets of Hong Kong and South Korea. As margin
calls came due and investors sold shares to cover severe liquidity needs
in Western markets, capital fled Asia, battering regional equities.
Moreover, as Western banks began to deleverage, reducing their $2.8 tril-
lion of credit to Asia, dollar liquidity dried up, along with interbank
markets and trade finance.

Although Asia's foreign-exchange position has strengthened dramatically over the past decade, the sudden shift in foreign financing
and the portfolio flows back to the West generated large exchange-
rate shifts: currencies in India, South Korea, and other Asian
economies depreciated significantly—by over 40 percent relative to
the dollar in the case of the South Korean won. Adjustments of
this magnitude caused significant losses on currency-hedging products,
especially among Asia's export-oriented small and midsize enterprises. Such losses, combined with the freezing of trade finance and
other serious liquidity issues, began to force some of these companies
into bankruptcy.

How should Asia respond? The answer will vary from economy to
economy and sector to sector. China and India, with their large

[1]See Stephen S. Roach, *Pitfalls in a Post-Bubble World*, Morgan Stanley, 2008.

and growing domestic markets, will find it easier to weather the storm than will mature economies, such as Japan, or late developers, such as Vietnam. Companies in domestically focused industries, such as telecommunications and health care, will do better than those in export-driven sectors, such as electronics and consumer goods.

Nonetheless, choices made in Asia—the source of a third of global GDP—will play a crucial role in driving a global recovery. We see three ways for the region to strengthen its own resilience and help the world recover from the crisis.

Boost demand at home

Many Asian countries have recently unveiled sweeping government spending plans; China's proposals, on the surface, appear to be the most ambitious. This is a region with huge infrastructure needs— especially in China and India and, to a lesser extent, Vietnam. Efforts to develop India's infrastructure are critical but may stall because of the tightening of credit and the weak finances of local governments. These efforts should be pursued aggressively to promote even faster growth through more rapid urbanization, much needed productivity improvements, and the multiplier effects of spending.

Asia is home to an enormous emerging middle class, which we esti- mate will grow by more than 800 million people within the next decade. Regional policy makers must do more—now—to unlock the spending power of this formidable group. In China, for example, private consumption accounts for only 35 percent of GDP, compared with more than 70 percent in the United States. Consumption- boosting measures, such as increased spending on social services, the liberalization of property rights, and wider access to consumer finance, will speed China's progress down the path of sustainable growth.

Accelerate intraregional trade and investment

Over the past seven years, trade within Asia has risen 75 percent faster than its trade with Europe and the United States. In fact, trade with the West is now half that of intra-Asian trade. Much of the growth, though, has come from the regional expansion of global supply chains culminating in Western markets. Asia's economies, with their burgeoning middle-class populations, must begin to see each other as end markets rather than only primarily as links in the global supply chain.

With negotiations over the Doha free-trade-development round stalled, Asian countries have shown new interest in regional free-trade agreements. More than 70 of them have been concluded among the ten members of the Association of Southeast Asian Nations (ASEAN), along with China, Japan, and South Korea.[2] Many more are under

---

[2] See Alan Wheatley, "Asia's infatuation with two-way trade saps WTO," *Reuters*, June 23, 2008.

negotiation. But such bilateral deals have far less impact on trade flows than regionwide agreements do. Asia's progress in liberalizing regional trade has been too slow, and it is imperative to rebuild momentum for a multilateral solution. The region's huge infrastructure needs and growing consumer class offer ample investment opportunities for Asian capital. More should be done to tap, for use within the region, the Asian savings and reserve funds allocated to sovereign wealth–style investments.

Strengthen local and regional financial markets
Asian financial markets have come a huge distance since 1997 but must evolve further if they are to continue supporting the region's growth over the next five years. More can be done to deepen local and regional capital markets, but in a measured way that seeks to avoid the excesses that have roiled those in the West. Pension reform would provide additional long-term local capital for domestic investment. Asia must do more to put in place the right consumer-finance credit regulations and infrastructure—such as credit bureaus to ensure that the emerging consumer class can spend more, but prudently. The region could also benefit from the adoption of countercyclical financial safeguards, such as dynamic provisioning (which requires banks to build rainy-day reserves in good times for future nonperforming loans) and dynamic capital-adequacy ratios (which would increase capital requirements in boom times and reduce them in troubled ones).

These efforts alone will not suffice. When leaders from Asian and European nations gathered in Beijing last October for their annual summit, several Asian participants called for the establishment of new regional financial institutions to promote growth and stability. Thailand urged the creation of an Asian version of the International Monetary Fund, to be capitalized with $350 billion. Leaders from the Philippines and South Korea offered similar proposals and urged broader currency-swap arrangements. Such ideas are worth exploring.

In the short term, though, Asia is likelier to achieve consensus by focusing on more targeted measures. These include developing the region's bond markets aggressively, consolidating its stock exchanges, and establishing additional mechanisms for improving the consistency and approach of regional regulators.

We welcome your comments on this article. Please send them to quarterly_comments@ mckinsey.com.

Each of these solutions implies a capacity for coordinated action that has thus far eluded Asia. The received wisdom has long been that it is too economically and politically diverse to integrate policy in a meaningful way. European-style cooperation may not be a realistic goal. Even so, current global financial problems give the region's leaders a unique opportunity to pull together. Asia isn't the source of the crisis but could point the way to its long-term resolution. ▸

Center Stage

A look at current trends and topics in management

How poor metrics undermine digital marketing

Jacques Bughin, Amy Guggenheim Shenkan, and Marc Singer

The Web has developed faster than the tools needed to analyze it have, so marketers have difficulty fully realizing the promise of history's most targetable and measurable medium. A June 2008 McKinsey digital-advertising survey of 340 senior marketing executives around the world shows what is—and isn't—happening.

Ninety-one percent of these executives report that their companies are advertising online. Many are experimenting with Web 2.0 vehicles. Yet 80 percent of our respondents say that their companies allocate media budgets by making subjective judgments or repeating whatever they did the previous year. Only half of the respondents' companies use even the most fundamental metric—click-through rates—to evaluate the impact of online direct-response ads. Only 30 percent consider the offline impact of online marketing, though a 2007 McKinsey study of 3,000 European broadband users showed that consumers are increasingly apt to combine online research with offline purchasing and vice versa. Purchases made strictly through one channel make up less than a third of the total. In many categories, the European study found, offline sales driven by online activity plus online sales driven by offline activity together represented an amount roughly equal to total online sales (exhibit).

There are signs of progress in measuring the effectiveness of online ads. A home-furnishings chain, for example, used a metric called RCQ (reach, cost, and quality) to optimize its allocation of spending among ad vehicles. Combining rigorous analytics with systematically applied judgment, RCQ not only

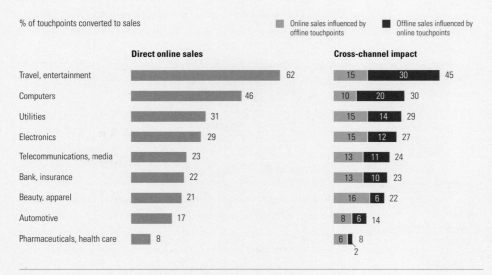

% of touchpoints converted to sales

■ Online sales influenced by offline touchpoints ■ Offline sales influenced by online touchpoints

Direct online sales

Travel, entertainment	62
Computers	46
Utilities	31
Electronics	29
Telecommunications, media	23
Bank, insurance	22
Beauty, apparel	21
Automotive	17
Pharmaceuticals, health care	8

Cross-channel impact

	Online	Offline	Total
Travel, entertainment	15	30	45
Computers	10	20	30
Utilities	15	14	29
Electronics	15	12	27
Telecommunications, media	13	11	24
Bank, insurance	13	10	23
Beauty, apparel	16	6	22
Automotive	8	6	14
Pharmaceuticals, health care	6	2	8

Source: 2008 McKinsey European customer-touchpoint survey

Artwork by Lloyd Miller

measures the number of people each ad vehicle reaches and the cost of reaching them through it but also includes a quality factor for changes in engagement, attitudes, and behavior. The analysis showed that the chain spent too much on work-horse vehicles, such as direct mail, and too little on TV infomercials (which convey more information) and online ads (which can be targeted more precisely).

Meanwhile, some retailers are trying out quantitative ways to assess the impact of on- and offline ads in other sales channels. To track results across them, one specialty retailer used online coupons redeemable on its Web site and in stores. The test showed that online media promoted offline sales effectively: customers redeemed more than three-quarters of the coupons in stores. This finding led the retailer to shift its spending away from some traditional media, particularly newspaper circulars, to online vehicles. The ability to track the impact of all spending across channels continuously might be a few years away, but the payoff is clear.

Techniques for optimizing online ads have come even further. Instead of basing the optimization on the last click before a conversion—usually a branded paid-search term—some marketers have started to use the technology that manages online ad campaigns (the ad-serving platform) to assess the impact of all online touch points. This approach requires an understanding of response rates by customer segment in order to serve more relevant ads across third-party sites and a marketer's own.

Finally, businesses are starting to exploit the promise of social media. One telecom company, for example, learned how to retain phone customers by assessing the strength of relationships among them. It used call patterns, changing call volumes, types of payment (prepaid or contract), handset types, and other traits to identify customers likely to depart and then constructed a diagram of their social ties, derived from the people they called, the people those people called, and how often. Generally, the more closely anyone was connected to a lost subscriber, the more

likely that person was to unsubscribe in turn. These techniques helped the telco improve its churn prediction model by 50 percent. What's more, by identifying the most influential potential churners and offering them new services and price plans, the company not only retained a quarter of these customers but also reduced the churn rate within their social networks by almost 40 percent.

Online media have enjoyed tremendous growth, but it will be far more robust if marketers learn the true impact of ads by using rigorous, accurate measurement techniques. Survey respondents whose companies have done so report greater satisfaction with digital marketing. In fact, 55 percent of them are cutting their spending on traditional media in order to increase funding for online ones, compared with only 43 percent of other companies.

Jacques Bughin is a director in McKinsey's Brussels office; **Amy Guggenheim Shenkan** is a consultant in the San Francisco office, where **Marc Singer** is a director.

The full version of this article is available on mckinseyquarterly.com.

From lean to lasting: Making operational improvements stick

By focusing on the "soft" side of lean and Six Sigma initiatives, leading global companies gain substantial, scalable, and sustainable advantages.

David Fine, Maia A. Hansen, and Stefan Roggenhofer

For companies seeking large-scale operational improvements, all roads lead to Toyota. Each year, thousands of executives tour its facilities to learn how lean production—the operational and organizational innovations the automaker pioneered—might help their own companies. During the past 20 years, lean has become, along with Six Sigma, one of two kinds of prominent performance-improvement programs adopted by global manufacturing and, more recently, service companies. Recently, organizations as diverse as steelmakers, insurance companies, and public-sector agencies have benefited from "leaning" their operations with Toyota's now-classic approach: eliminating waste, variability, and inflexibility.

Yet in our experience, organizations overlook up to half of the potential savings when they implement or expand operational-improvement programs inspired by lean, Six Sigma, or both.[1] Some companies set their sights too low; others falter by implementing lean and other performance-enhancing tools without recognizing how existing performance-management systems or employee mind-sets might undermine them. Still others underestimate the level of senior-management involvement required; for example, they delegate responsibility for change programs to their lean experts or Six Sigma black belts—practitioners who are technically skilled but often lack the authority, capabilities, or numbers to make change stick.

[1] While lean and Six Sigma are distinct methodologies, many companies combine elements of the two. In this article, we outline best practices that are equally fruitful in lean, Six Sigma, and related hybrid environments rather than advocate one approach over the other.

Josh Cochran

The broader challenge underlying such problems is integrating the better-known "hard" operational tools and approaches—such as just-in-time production—with the "soft" side, including the development of leaders who can help teams to continuously identify and make efficiency improvements, link and align the boardroom with the shop floor, and build the technical and interpersonal skills that make efficiency benefits real. Mastering lean's softer side is difficult because it forces all employees to commit themselves to new ways of thinking and working. Toyota remains the exemplar: while many companies can replicate its lean technology, success on the softer side often eludes them.

Some companies, however, overcome the challenges and get more from their operational-improvement programs. Against a backdrop of growing economic uncertainty, their success can be a source of inspiration and enlightenment for industrial and service companies and for public- and social-sector organizations looking to extract greater value from these efforts.

Soft is hard

Making operational change stick is difficult. Operations typically account for the largest number of a company's employees and the widest variation

A better approach to scaling

The task of rolling out a performance transformation program across a company's global operations—with thousands or even tens of thousands of workers—presents big challenges, which are particularly evident in attempts to scale up successful pilots. Many companies are tempted to undertake everything simultaneously, often by launching a frenzy of loosely related kaizen[1] projects across many operating units and by relying on broadly themed, company-wide training programs to instill the new philosophy of continuous improvement.

This approach seldom succeeds: its inherent lack of coordination leads to an uneven pattern of implementation, which often feels confusing or contradictory to workers. Likewise, enthusiasm often wanes when workers, who may receive training months before they apply it, come to view the program as distracting. While this approach almost always introduces useful skills and tools, its disjointed application subtly encourages workers, and even some leaders, to see training rather than business results as the real objective.

When companies tackle implementation in a more coordinated way, they get bigger, more sustainable results. The key is to start with just one or two operating areas and transform their performance completely, in essence creating the building blocks to be replicated throughout the company. This approach focuses management's attention on the program and thereby helps ensure that its elements, such as technical changes and training, are sequenced properly to avoid confusing employees.

These building blocks, or "minitransformations," can be much larger than typical kaizen projects if the operating areas involved have logical boundaries—for example, a production line in a large plant, everything within the walls of a small plant, or all operations associated with a particular customer. We suggest choosing areas with about 100 to 200 employees, as projects of this size are small enough to manage effectively yet large enough to generate the high levels of enthusiasm and organizational energy that help sustain large-scale change.[2]

An additional sidebar, "Managers have feelings too," is available on mckinseyquarterly.com.

in skill levels. Units often are scattered across dozens or even hundreds of sites throughout the world, function independently, and have distinct corporate cultures—particularly if M&A has fueled a company's growth. Each facility may specialize in different products or services and face unique pressures from customers, competitors, and regulators. These factors complicate efforts to design, execute, and scale operational-improvement programs (see sidebar, "A better approach to scaling").

Consequently, many companies emphasize the technical aspects of their programs over the organizational ones. That approach is understandable. Technical solutions are objective and straightforward; analytical solutions to operational problems abound in lean and Six Sigma tool kits; and companies make significant investments to train experts who know how to apply them. What's more, the tools and experts actually are invaluable in diagnosing and improving operational performance.

Overlooking the softer side, however, drastically lowers any initiative's odds of success. Some companies, for example, rush to implement the tool kit without ensuring that their employees—including managers—are prepared to work and lead in new and different ways. In such cases, "initiative fatigue"

A global IT services company took that kind of approach when it first scaled up its pilot effort, choosing to focus on all operational activities associated with serving an important customer. To ramp up the program quickly, while taking care not to jeopardize the results by overextending the company's people, senior executives used this first expansion of the pilot as a training ground for the leaders of subsequent ones: the line managers and lean-team members who would run the second and third waves (extending the program to cover a second and third customer, respectively) were included in the first wave. This "pull forward" approach, supported by a project team at the corporate center to ensure consistency, helped the company extend the initiative to more than 100 global customer accounts in just 18 months. In addition to improving customer satisfaction significantly, the company substantially lowered its labor costs and raised labor productivity by more than 40 percent.

Of course, some elements of an improvement program must be instituted at the company-wide level;

a single production line, for example, shouldn't have its own performance-management system. By taking a more coordinated approach to implementation, senior executives can concentrate attention on these and other cross-cutting initiatives (say, a new IT system or compensation scheme, or even special career paths for employees who leave their line positions to assist in company-wide scaling activities over many months). By approaching implementation in this fashion, with cross-cutting initiatives serving as the mortar holding together the building blocks of the program, top companies minimize the chances that poor timing or unanticipated events will return employees to the firefighting mode that characterized the old ways of working.

Stephen Corbett and Maia A. Hansen

Stephen Corbett is a principal in McKinsey's Toronto office, and **Maia Hansen** is a principal in the Cleveland office.

[1] Continuous improvement.
[2] Organizational (or human) energy is the willingness and ability to adopt new, value-creating forms of behavior. For more about the role of energy in performance transformations, see Josep Isern and Caroline Pung, "Driving radical change," mckinseyquarterly.com, November 2007.

and even distrust may set in, and efficiency gains fizzle out as the black belts move on to other projects.

At times, such an improvement initiative first appears to be successful but is later found to be insufficient to meet the company's main objectives. An aerospace manufacturer, for example, wanted to increase managing of a product with rapidly growing sales. The company's lean experts, assigned to plan and run the initiative, quickly identified productivity-enhancement opportunities and began conducting *kaizen* projects.[2] On the surface, the program was working: the number of projects and employees trained in the new approaches—two indicators the company tracked—were increasing. But management's inattention to the softer side created difficulties.

Since the program's goals weren't adequately defined or communicated by senior managers, the experts focused on what they could achieve— primarily easy wins, including technical changes to redesign assembly processes and to improve the effectiveness of certain machines. In retrospect, these changes, while broadly useful, did little to help meet growing demand for the product. Meanwhile, some of the company's salespeople, long frustrated with what they saw as the shortcomings of the operations group, began circumventing the production-scheduling system in order to speed their own products through the queue. That undercut many of the efficiency gains the experts managed to create.

The result, in fact, was chaos: line workers later showed executives a schedule indicating that one machine, chosen at random, was to perform 250 hours of work during an 8-hour shift. This revelation spurred the executives to refocus the program, investigate the organizational factors behind the difficulties, and ultimately identify much more far-reaching solutions—starting with an effort to get sales and operations to collaborate in setting production priorities and to work together on a daily basis.

Getting started: Set high aspirations

Such examples show that neglecting the organizational components of an operational transformation can delay or even derail it. Top companies, by contrast, attend to the softer elements of an initiative throughout its whole course, starting with the earliest, aspiration-setting phases, when senior leaders identify the key goals and start to communicate them. That helps companies to establish a stronger foundation for change and to set more achievable, and often much higher, ambitions than they otherwise could.

[2] Rapid, concentrated projects aimed at making continuous, incremental, small-scale process improvements at the line level.

A better understanding of the cultural starting point enables top companies to determine where they should focus at the beginning of a program, when to implement its various elements, and how to achieve their goals.

Consider the experience of a North American power generator that used cultural insights to combat skepticism about the scope of the efficiency improvements attainable in a nascent initiative. This kind of doubt is common when companies lack a self-evident catalyst for change—say, a takeover or a looming bankruptcy. The power generator responded by sending its managers to visit a company, in another process-intensive industry, that had recently implemented a lean program. There the managers saw similar improvements in action and heard the enthusiasm that line managers and union leaders expressed for them. That experience was instrumental in helping the managers address their own employees' uncertainties about how much improvement was possible.

Likewise, greater attention to corporate culture helped a global chemical company launch an efficiency-improvement program across its network of 300 plants. The company's abiding respect for science and for highly educated experts at first biased managers in favor of solutions based on new technology rather than line-level process improvements. After conducting a pilot project, however, executives saw that about 60 percent of the value it generated came from new work processes, not new and more efficient machines. That realization changed the design of the program and raised its goals—in some cases, by a factor of three. The company now expects the program to have an annual impact of more than $1 billion.

By contrast, companies that misread employee mind-sets and other cultural elements squander time and resources. A large logistics group that tried to overhaul its transport network, for example, overlooked the way years of inadequate capital investment would affect the program's ramp-up. Why did the company make this mistake? It turned out that the gradual decline in capital spending had, over time, led the company's maintenance workers to assume that their skills weren't valued, so the seriousness of many problems had gone unreported. The company's executives found that the goals of the program were therefore initially unattainable.

Making change happen
After accounting for the way culture and other organizational factors will affect the goals of a program, leading companies put what they learn into action. They reap bigger, more sustainable benefits by balancing the program's hard and soft elements and developing their line managers' lean-leadership skills.

Take a balanced approach

The experience of a North American distribution company that sought to address higher customer expectations and eroding margins in its network of 70 distribution centers shows the virtues of a more balanced approach (Exhibit 1). The company looked beyond technical changes, to the ways that organizational structures and processes—and even the mind-sets of employees—could affect its ability to meet the goals it set.

Operations leaders identified labor balancing as an important technical improvement: they planned to create teams that would combine two roles—"pickers," who located products to fill customer orders, and "packers," who loaded orders onto trucks. The new system was supposed to increase productivity by redistributing labor more efficiently to meet shifting demand. The company didn't stop at such technical fixes, however. In parallel, it revamped its performance-management system to encourage the new ways of working. Pickers had been measured quantitatively (primarily on speed, not accuracy), packers qualitatively or not at all, depending on the site. Executives now combined the existing metrics into a team-based system aimed at helping the company's trucks depart on time. This change not only balanced speed and accuracy but also pushed workers to collaborate and to focus on a common goal. In addition, the company created a prominent visual tracking system to reinforce the new behavior by showing employees, in real time, when shifting workloads required their immediate attention.

Changing the mind-sets of workers proved critical as well. Many workers in both groups, which had viewed each other as rivals, were company veterans who strongly identified with their roles. Pickers had traditionally felt superior, since they typically worked alone and could be quite successful with individualized approaches, whereas packing was more standardized. Recognizing that such factors would breed resentment if ignored, the company provided supervisors with on-the-job training in interpersonal skills—including coaching and the art of having difficult conversations—in the weeks before making the technical changes. The supervisors later reported that the integration and timing of these elements helped the program succeed by instilling in them the influencing skills needed to highlight the new system's benefits (both to their teams and to individual workers) and to convince doubters that the changes were important. (Often, companies undermine their performance-improvement programs by introducing otherwise useful training elements at inappropriate times—for instance, several months before the implementation of the program, when its goals may not be clear to the trainees.)

Within six months, the distribution centers that had adopted the new system were 10 to 15 percent more productive, on-time deliveries were up 5 to 10 percent, and errors reported by customers were down by as much as one-

EXHIBIT 1

A balanced approach

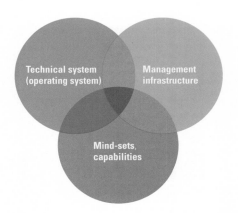

The way corporate resources are deployed
to meet customer needs at lowest costs
- Production planning, logistics systems
- Quality systems, processes
- Labor allocation
- Maintenance systems, processes

The way formal structures and processes
are used to manage technical systems and
achieve business objectives
- Performance management
- Talent management (eg, recruiting, career paths,
  compensation)
- Organizational design, roles, responsibilities

The way people think and feel about their work
and conduct themselves in their workplace
- Leadership alignment, role modeling
- Clear direction, compelling purpose
- Discipline, collaboration, accountability, trust
- Focus on continuous improvement
- Effective individual skills

third. Moreover, a survey of workers found that their satisfaction levels had risen by 10 percent. Subsequent analysis suggested that about half of the productivity gains were attributable to the softer elements and about half to technical changes, such as more efficient warehouse layouts.

Lead through the line

At the heart of most big operational-improvement efforts are a company's black belts, lean sensei, and other change agents brought in to lead programs, spur new ideas and practices, and champion the mind-set of continuous improvement. Companies typically follow this template because it appears easier than significantly involving their line leadership. Shop floor deadlines are fierce, line leaders are busy, and many of them lack the skills to direct large initiatives. Some executives therefore argue that line managers should focus instead on day-to-day concerns.

Yet that is a mistake. Large-scale change requires all employees—from the C-suite to the shop floor—to think and work differently (Exhibit 2). Companies that use only experts to orchestrate change programs may be fairly successful. Still, by outsourcing the responsibility for initiatives (and, by extension, the underlying ideas) to experts, even their own, these companies often miss significant opportunities. Moreover, once the low-hanging fruit is gone, such efforts often lose steam as employees slip into old habits; experts may convey the new language or technical tools but rarely the desire to change behavior permanently, nor can these experts build the organizational capabilities that permanent change requires.

By contrast, when a company shifts the attention of its line managers away from firefighting, develops their leadership capabilities, and expects more from them, the gains are bigger and longer lasting. Experts still play a vital catalyzing role, of course, but now as teachers, coaches, and counselors. Line managers are better placed to lead change efforts and to serve as long-term role models—and should be held accountable for doing so.

The North American power generator mentioned previously learned this lesson several months into its improvement initiative as executives sought to fire up the program's momentum. This company had sent its operations experts into field offices, so they could work closely with employees at individual plants, where they had enjoyed significant success.

Senior executives, however, observed that enthusiasm and engagement soon started fading among the line workers. In the words of one executive, "They were still coming to work from the neck down." Senior executives therefore vowed to move the effort "out of the office and into the line." The company created a "lean leader" profile—a list of desirable characteristics, such as problem-solving, coaching, and analytical skills. Management then created a curriculum to build them through the "forum and field" approach: hands-on training and coaching forums (on topics such as performance management, time management, and problem solving) followed by practice in real-world applications.

Related articles on mckinseyquarterly.com

Driving radical change

Creating organizational transformations:
McKinsey Global Survey Results

Beyond manufacturing: The evolution of lean production

To ensure that everyone understood the permanence of the changes, the company made weekly one-on-one training and coaching sessions a part of its line managers' jobs. Shift schedules were adjusted to incorporate coaching into the workers' routines. (While most executives recognize the value of coaching, many fail to institutionalize it, thus unintentionally making it seem less important.) These brief sessions allowed workers to celebrate successes, share ideas, and measure progress in achieving the program's goals. Soon, employees began carrying index cards listing the improvement priorities they had spotted during the previous week.

The cards and related conversations generated creative ideas—including a new way to keep coal dry when it was shipped to the company's power plants. These and other line-led improvements helped significantly to raise the plant's output and, subsequently, to cut its fuel costs. More important,

EXHIBIT 2

Six habits of lean leaders

Employees can't change if their managers don't. Lean leaders act as role models for the mind-sets and behavior they wish to instill in their teams.

Habit	Example
1. A focus on operating processes: Senior managers use visible activities to demonstrate the importance of process and of making standardization a habit.	*The COO conducts regular shop floor visits and Q&As to review milling-machine operating processes and reinforce standards with workers.*
2. Root cause problem solving: Managers fight the instinct to provide immediate solutions to problems, instead using them as teaching opportunities.	*Responding to an unanticipated problem, a brewery plant manager first ensures that proper containment measures are taken, and then challenges the team to analyze causes—using the "five why" method (examination of a problem to uncover the underlying cause).*
3. Clear performance expectations: Transparent performance dialogues take place at all levels of management.	*An insurance company's frontline employees meet for 10 minutes daily with their team leaders to track productivity and discuss improvement ideas. Productivity metrics are tracked visually and displayed prominently.*
4. Aligned leadership: Process improvements don't stop at functional boundaries.	*To create a more open and collaborative environment, the COO ties half of the functional leaders' year-end bonuses to the key performance indicators (KPIs) of the entire management team.*
5. A sense of purpose: Connections between day-to-day work and compelling, long-term aspirations become tangible throughout the company.	*To make goals tangible in its quality-improvement program, a medical-products maker brings in health experts to show frontline workers how products are used in surgery—thus emphasizing the importance of meeting quality objectives.*
6. Support for people: Managers recognize and demonstrate that frontline workers are a source of customer value. These workers are empowered and encouraged to make important decisions.	*An area sales manager drives to the head office to pick up a replacement printer that frontline agents need to continue working efficiently.*

the training efforts enhanced the skills of managers, enabling them to become the foundation for a host of additional improvements.

To get the most from large operational-improvement programs, top companies look beyond the technical aspects of lean and Six Sigma and embrace the softer side. Complementing the development of technical skills with a focus on the organizational capabilities that make efficiency benefits real can help companies to achieve more substantial, sustainable, and scalable results. Q

The authors wish to acknowledge the contributions of Chinta Bhagat, Steve Bonz, Mallory Caldwell, Stephen Corbett, Aaron DeSmet, Amanda Hansen, Tom Janssens, Robert Lewis, Jeff Moore, Mikael Robertson, Jason Weddingfeld, Sarah Wilson, and Carter Wood.

•

David Fine is a director in McKinsey's Johannesburg office, **Maia Hansen** is a principal in the Cleveland office, and **Stefan Roggenhofer** is a principal in the Munich office.

We welcome your comments on this article.
Please send them to quarterly_comments@mckinsey.com.

Why baby boomers will need to **work longer**

Most US baby boomers are not prepared for their retirement, and neither are the US and world economies. Boomers can help mitigate the consequences by remaining in the workforce beyond the traditional retirement age.

Eric D. Beinhocker, Diana Farrell, and Ezra Greenberg

The twilight of the US baby boom generation is approaching, and with it deep, structural economic shifts whose impact will be felt for decades to come.[1] New research from the McKinsey Global Institute (MGI) shows that there is only one realistic way to prevent aging boomers from experiencing a significant decline in their living standards and becoming a multidecade drag on US and world economic growth. Boomers will have to continue working beyond the traditional retirement age, and that will require important changes in public policy, business practices, and personal behavior. These adjustments have become even more urgent with the recent financial turmoil, which has sharply reduced the home values and financial investments of millions of boomers just as they approach retirement.

Underlying the need for change is a reversal of trends that have been in operation since the 1960s. For decades, boomers swelled the ranks of the US labor force, driving up economic output as they earned and consumed more than any other generation in history. Now, as the boomers age and retire, US labor force participation rates are declining. Without an unexpected burst of productivity growth or a significant upsurge in investment per worker, the aging boomers' reduced levels of working and spending will slow the real growth of the US GDP from an average of 3.2 percent a year since 1965

Bill Butcher

---

[1] We define baby boomers as people born in the years from 1945 through 1964.

to about 2.4 percent over the next three decades. That long-term growth rate is 25 percent lower than the one the United States and the world have long taken for granted.

MGI research highlights a further problem: two-thirds of the oldest boomers are financially unprepared for retirement, and many are not even aware of their predicament.[2] This lack of sufficient resources will not only mean a less comfortable retirement for tens of millions of households but also depress spending in the overall economy.

Yet the boomers' retirement need not be such a major dislocation. We estimate that a two-year increase in the median retirement age over the next decade would add almost $13 trillion to real US GDP during the next 30 years while cutting roughly in half the number of boomers who would be financially unprepared for retirement.

Our research shows that many boomers actually do want to continue working. Nonetheless, a number of institutional and legal barriers—health care costs, labor laws, pension regulations, and corporate attitudes toward older workers—could prevent them from prolonging their careers. Overcoming these barriers will require the government to reallocate health insurance costs for older workers, businesses and boomers to agree on more flexible work arrangements, policy makers to reform private pensions, and Social Security to remove disincentives to remaining in the workforce.

We reached these conclusions by combining three complementary research methods. First, MGI surveyed 5,100 households with members aged 50 to 70 to better understand and compare the attitudes of boomers and members of the previous "silent" generation toward aging, retirement, saving, consumption, and work. Second, we assembled a comprehensive database of boomer household finances and collected similar data for the preceding and following generations. Third, we used the survey and the database to build an economic model that projects boomer household finances through 2035 and to study how their evolution would affect the wider economy.

Last year, MGI and our colleagues in McKinsey's marketing practice drew on this research to show business leaders how they should prepare for the changing needs of older boomers.[3] In this article, we examine the implications for the living standards of boomer households and for the economy as a whole.

---

[2] For both the baby boomers and other generations, we distinguish between the early members (born during the first ten years) and the late members (born in the subsequent decade).

[3] See David Court, Diana Farrell, and John E. Forsyth, "Serving aging baby boomers," mckinseyquarterly.com, November 2007.

One-time factors that boosted boomers' incomes

The basic facts about the baby boomers are well known. This age cohort (79 million strong) ranks as the richest in US history; is 50 percent larger than the silent generation, which preceded it; and represented, at the time of its birth, a larger share of the US population than the succeeding cohorts (Generation X and the Millennials) did at the time of theirs.[4]

Far less well understood are the reasons for this generation's economic success. Boomers have collectively earned more than twice as much as members of the silent generation did at the same age—$3.7 trillion versus $1.6 trillion (Exhibit 1). Our research shows that 80 percent of the difference resulted from three factors quite specific to the boomers. (The remaining 20 percent reflected economic growth from which the boomers benefited as much as other generations did over their working lives.)

The first exceptional source of these income gains was the boomer cohort's sheer size, which raised output and growth rates. Second, the boomers lived quite differently from the way previous generations did. As women

[4] Members of the silent generation were born in the years from 1925 to 1945, Generation Xers from 1965 to 1984, and the Millennials from 1985 to 2004.

EXHIBIT 1

Baby, you're a rich man

Drivers of change in total income, by US age cohorts,[1] $ billion (in real 2000 dollars)

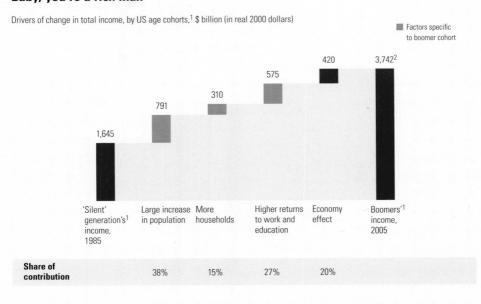

■ Factors specific to boomer cohort

1,645	791	310	575	420	3,742[2]

'Silent' generation's[1] income, 1985 — Large increase in population — More households — Higher returns to work and education — Economy effect — Boomers'[1] income, 2005

| Share of contribution | 38% | 15% | 27% | 20% | |

[1] Silent generation = people born between 1925 and 1945; boomers = those born from 1945 through 1964; age refers to cohort midpoint.
[2] Figures do not sum to total, because of rounding.

Source: McKinsey Global Institute analysis

poured into the workplace and social mores changed, boomers married and had children later, as well as divorced and remained single at higher rates. These changes in turn raised the number of households and therefore the number of wage earners relative to the total population. Third, boomers had higher returns to both education and work at a time when the labor force was shifting from industrial to service and knowledge jobs. In particular, the boomers' higher levels of education enabled them to capitalize over the course of their careers—to a degree greater than other generations did—on economic changes stemming from productivity growth, technological innovation, and globalization.

In all likelihood, the factors driving the boomers' exceptional income growth won't recur. Subsequent generations, though large in numbers, represent a smaller share of the total population; the size of households has stabilized; and gains in educational attainment and the workforce participation rates of women have largely topped out.

The implications for growth

The aging of the boomers won't just slow income growth. As the population ages, fewer people will be working. The result will be falling labor force participation rates, which are a critical factor in determining GDP growth (economic output is largely a function of the labor and capital available in an economy and of its productivity in using those inputs).

When the boomers first began entering the US workforce, participation rates rose significantly, from 59 percent in 1965 to 65 percent by 1985, peaking at 67 percent from 1995 to 2000. This surge contributed significantly to the 3.2 percent average annual real GDP growth that the United States enjoyed from 1965 to 2006.

Labor force participation has declined to 66 percent today and is headed, according to our research, toward 60 percent by 2035—a level not seen since the 1960s. If labor productivity and capital growth continue on current trends, declining labor force participation will knock real GDP growth down to 2.6 percent from 2007 to 2016, to 2.4 percent from 2017 to 2026, and to 2.2 percent from 2027 to 2035. A slowdown of this magnitude would represent a structural shift for the US economy and leave it with growth rates typical of Europe's in recent decades.

Lifetime savings and earnings patterns

The fact that boomers have consumed more and saved less during their working lives than previous generations did compounds the demographic challenge for the US economy (Exhibit 2). Typically, households accumulate savings at an accelerating rate, reaching a peak during their prime earning years. They subsequently draw down those savings in retirement. The collective savings rate of the boomers, however, didn't peak during their prime earning years. In fact, the missing boomer peak accounts for most of the collapse in the US household savings rate from its high of more than 10 percent, in the mid-1980s, to about 2 percent today.[5]

This dramatic change in savings behavior had a number of causes. Soaring stock markets and home prices made the boomers feel richer and thus diminished any sense of urgency they might have felt to save. The increased availability of credit and low interest rates made it easier to borrow. And boomer attitudes toward savings were different from those of the silent generation, born amid the deprivations of the Depression and World War II. Even before the recent credit crunch, the boomers' ratio of debt to net worth was 50 percent higher than the silent generation's at the same age. Sharply declining house prices have caused this measure of boomer indebtedness to surge.

Unprepared and unaware

The low savings rate and extensive liabilities of the boomers have left about two-thirds of them unprepared for retirement. We reached this conclusion

[5] In 2005, the boomers had 47 percent of all disposable income but contributed only seven percentage points to overall household savings.

EXHIBIT 2

Running on empty

US age cohorts[1]

—— Early boomers   —— Early 'silent' generation
—— Late boomers   —— Late 'silent' generation   ▲→ Forecast

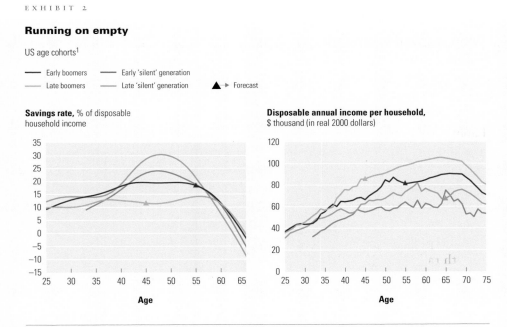

Savings rate, % of disposable household income

Disposable annual income per household, $ thousand (in real 2000 dollars)

[1] Silent generation = people born between 1925 and 1945; boomers = those born from 1945 through 1964; early = those born in first 10 years, late = those born in subsequent decade. Compares 10-year cohorts at same age: early boomers vs early members of silent generation at age 55; late boomers vs late members of silent generation at age 45. Age refers to cohort midpoint.

Source: McKinsey Global Institute analysis

by assessing the level of postretirement income and assets that the boomers would need to maintain 80 percent of their peak preretirement spending.[6] This analysis—based on net financial assets such as bank deposits, stocks, and bonds, minus credit card balances, car loans, and other nonmortgage debt—indicates that 69 percent of the boomers are not prepared to maintain their lifestyles. The inclusion of home equity, whose value is declining in many regions below the levels prevailing when we undertook our analysis, only reduces the proportion of the unprepared to 62 percent.

This lack of financial preparation will affect not just the poor, who have always struggled with retirement, but large numbers of middle-class Americans as well. Less than half of boomer households earning $60,000 to $90,000 a year are prepared, even if home equity values before the credit crunch are included in their assets.

Many are not even aware of their predicament. In our survey, about half of boomer households expressed confidence in their financial future. But by our calculations, less than half of those confident households are adequately prepared.

The boomers have always been an adaptable generation, and there's no reason to believe that their resourcefulness will disappear as they age. Still, the sheer number of unprepared, unaware boomers suggests that many of them face a difficult economic adjustment in the years ahead.

Working and saving longer

The single most important step that unprepared boomers can take to improve their financial well-being is to postpone retirement and the draw-down of their savings. If they worked long enough to increase the median retirement age from 62.6 today to 64.1 by 2015, they could continue accumulating assets longer and avoid tapping them until age 70. That combination would dramatically reduce the share of unprepared households—to 40 percent, from 69 percent, if households don't tap their home equity, and to 31 percent, from 62 percent, if they do. Although that increase in the median retirement age may not sound like much, it typically shifts slowly; in fact, it took three decades (from 1970 to 2000) to fall by the same amount. The challenge now is to reverse that trend, but much more rapidly.

Higher rates of labor force participation as a result of longer careers would also significantly raise overall growth in the economy, generating $12.9 trillion more in GDP from now until 2035 than would occur otherwise. Household savings in this new scenario would rise by $400 billion, increas-

[6] The figure of 80 percent is based on our model of life cycle spending patterns. This model shows that for the average early boomer, spending roughly doubles from the ages of 30 to 55, peaks at age 62, and then drops by about 20 percent over the course of retirement.

ing the overall savings rate to 5.4 percent by 2022—a jump of roughly three percentage points. Furthermore, boomers would pay more taxes and could delay drawing down government retirement benefits, therefore helping to ease the impact of aging on both Social Security and Medicare.

Willing but unable to work?

Eighty-five percent of the boomers we surveyed said that it was at least somewhat likely that they would continue to work beyond the traditional retirement age. Nearly 40 percent said that it was extremely likely, and of those, two-thirds emphasized financial reasons (Exhibit 3). This finding suggests that one explanation for the confidence of unprepared boomers is the belief that they will continue to earn a living longer than previous generations have.

Yet not all those saying they intend to work will be able to do so. Our survey found that half of the boomers who have retired early did so for health reasons. A majority live in lower-income, less-prepared households— precisely the people who most need to remain employed. Many boomers aren't knowledge workers: nearly half have physically stressful manufacturing, transport, and construction jobs, which they will have difficulty keeping later in life.

EXHIBIT 3

The long and winding road

Likelihood of returning to work, % of nonretired boomers

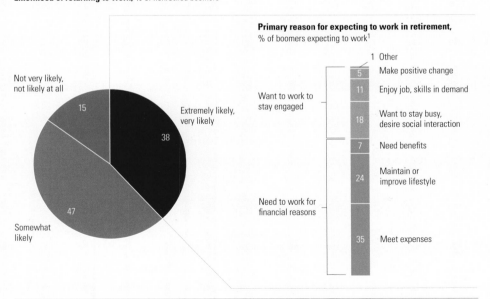

[1] Figures do not sum to 100%, because of rounding.

Source: 2007 McKinsey survey of aging US consumers

Finally, even those who maintain their health and want to continue working will find it difficult, as significant legal and institutional barriers remain. Policies related to insurance and Medicare, pensions and Social Security, and employment practices make it harder for businesses to employ older workers and for older workers to embrace longer careers.

Encouraging longer working lives

By adjusting policies affecting older workers, leaders in government and business can help boomers and the economy as a whole address the challenges of the coming transition. Policy makers and executives should pay particular attention to three critical priorities.

Reallocating health insurance costs

Health insurance costs rise with age, creating a disincentive for a business to retain or hire older workers. The situation becomes more complicated when they reach age 65. Unlike retirees, employees that age and older do not receive full Medicare benefits if they work for a company that has more than 20 people on staff and provides health benefits. The employer is viewed as the primary provider of coverage, and Medicare offers coverage only for services not included in the employer's plans. The reluctance of companies to bear health insurance costs thus impedes the hiring of older workers. Offering full Medicare coverage to all people age 65 and older, regardless of employment status, would eliminate this disincentive. Although taxes to finance Medicare would rise, the added tax revenue from older workers remaining in employment would partially offset that increase. The broader economy would gain from having more older workers.

Related articles on mckinseyquarterly.com

Taking the risk out of retirement

What US workers don't know about retirement

Serving aging baby boomers

Enabling businesses to offer flexible work arrangements

Many boomers say they are willing to continue working if they can do so part time, work from home, or make arrangements that would cut their hours and pay gradually. Government and educational institutions use such practices today; businesses have held back, partly out of concern that they might violate federal laws on taxes, pensions, and age discrimination. Policy makers should act to alleviate such concerns. Meanwhile, businesses must develop an integrated strategy to employ mature workers— a strategy centered on more flexible arrangements. Workers, in return, will have to be flexible about pay and benefits.

Removing disincentives in Social Security and private pensions
Although the Pension Protection Act of 2006 and recent modifications to
Social Security have reduced some disincentives for working later in life,
further reform is needed. Under current law, for example, the one-third
of boomer households covered by defined-benefit plans can begin receiving pensions at the age of 59.5 if the wage earner in the household stops
working. Continued part-time work delays the start of eligibility for
receiving pension payments until age 62. Lowering that age would reduce
this disincentive.

Similarly, lawmakers should examine the way Social Security retirement
benefits are calculated. Currently, payments to retirees are based on their
35 highest-earning years. The practical implication is that working longer
typically provides only a modest increase in benefits, yet workers continue
to pay the full payroll tax during later years. An alternative would be
to base benefit calculations on a longer time period, such as 40 years, after
which workers would no longer owe payroll taxes. That kind of change
would create a stronger financial incentive to continue in employment.

In short, demographics need not be destiny. Government and business
leaders who start acting now to change policies and practices can lessen
the negative impact of the boomers' aging and help tens of millions of
households enjoy a more secure retirement. The boomers have reinvented
themselves and society throughout their lifetimes. They can reinvent
aging and retirement too. Q

The authors wish to acknowledge the contributions of Jonathan Ablett, Vivek Banerji,
Lora Chajka-Cadin, John Chao, David Court, John Forsyth, Vanessa Freeman, Geoffrey Greene,
Matt Klusas, Mette Lykke, Jeongyeon Shim, and Suruchi Shukla.

•

Eric Beinhocker is a senior fellow with the McKinsey Global Institute, where
Diana Farrell is director and **Ezra Greenberg** is a consultant. Copyright © 2009
McKinsey & Company. All rights reserved.

We welcome your comments on this article.
Please send them to quarterly_comments@mckinsey.com.

The full version of this article is available on mckinseyquarterly.com.

Getting into your
competitor's head

To anticipate the moves of your rivals, you must understand how their strategists and decision makers think.

**Hugh Courtney, John T. Horn,
and Jayanti Kar**

The global financial crisis that erupted in 2008 shows, with painful clarity, that we live in an interdependent business world. In bleak times and fair, the success of a company's strategy often depends greatly on the strategies of its competitors. In periods of financial turmoil, for instance, the prospects—and even survival—of a bank often depend on the near-term M&A of its rivals. Similarly, the ultimate success of Boeing's new commercial jet, the 787 Dreamliner, will depend on the way Airbus positions, markets, and sells its new and competing A380 and A350. Pfizer's ability to sustain market share and profitability in the market for cholesterol-lowering treatments will depend on the moves of the company's branded and generic pharmaceutical competitors, to say nothing of biotech and medical-product companies developing alternative treatments.

This strategic interdependence implies that the ability to anticipate your competitors' strategies is essential. Yet a recent survey of business executives found that the actions and reactions of potential rivals almost never play a role in, for example, decisions to introduce and price new products.[1] An important reason for this neglect, we believe, is that strategic-planning tools, such as game theory and scenario planning, are of limited use unless a company can correctly define the key elements of the strategic game,

[1] David Montgomery, Marian Chapman Moore, and Joel Urbany, "Reasoning about competitive reactions: Evidence from executives," *Marketing Science*, 2005, Volume 24, Number 1, pp. 138–49.

Keith Negley

especially the strategic options and objectives of competitors. This is no easy task. Rare is the company that truly understands what its competitors and their decision makers care about most, how they perceive their assets and capabilities, and what all this means for their strategies. A company with such insights could reverse-engineer the moves of competitors and predict what they were likely to do. In a credit crunch, for instance, such a company would be well positioned to buy financial and nonfinancial assets at attractive prices if it knew that poorly capitalized competitors would avoid new risk and therefore not bid for these assets.

Getting inside your competitor's head is difficult because companies (and their decision makers) usually are not alike. At any time, a company has assets, resources, market positions, and capabilities it must protect, leverage, and build upon. Different endowments imply different strategies even in the same general market environment. What's more, even a competitor with similar endowments may pursue different strategies if its owners, stakeholders, and decision makers have a different objective.

So if you want to anticipate rather than react to strategic moves, you must analyze a competitor at two levels: organizational and individual. At the organizational level, you have to think like a strategist of your competitor by searching for the perfect strategic fit between its endowments and its changing market environment. At the individual level, you have to think like the decision makers of the competitor, identifying who among them makes which decisions and the influences and incentives guiding their choices. This approach moves you beyond the data-gathering efforts of most competitive-intelligence functions, toward a thought process that helps turn competitive intelligence into competitive insights. While our approach won't eliminate surprises, it will help you better understand your competitors and their likely moves and eliminate some of the guesswork that undermines the development of strategies in an increasingly interdependent business world.

Think like your competitor's strategist

When your competitor resembles you, chances are it will pursue similar strategies—what we call symmetric competition. When companies have different assets, resources, capabilities, and market positions, they will probably react to the same market opportunities and threats in different ways—what we call asymmetric competition. One of the keys to predicting a competitor's future strategies is to understand how much or little it resembles your company.

In the fast-food industry, for example, two leading players, McDonald's and Burger King, face the same market trends but have responded in markedly different ways to the obesity backlash. McDonald's has rolled out a variety of foods it promotes as healthy. Burger King has introduced high-fat, high-calorie sandwiches supported by in-your-face, politically incorrect ads. As the dominant player, McDonald's is the lightning rod for the consumer and government backlash on obesity. It can't afford to thumb its nose at these concerns. Smaller players like Burger King, realizing this, see an opportunity to cherry-pick share in the less health-conscious fast-food segment. Burger King competes asymmetrically.

Companies can determine whether they face symmetric or asymmetric competition by using the resource-based view of strategy: the idea that they should protect, leverage, extend, build, or acquire resources and capabilities that are valuable, rare, and inimitable and that can be successfully exploited. Resources come in three categories: tangible assets (for example, physical, technological, financial, and human resources), intangible assets (brands, reputation, and knowledge), and current market positions (access to customers, economies of scale and scope, and experience). Capabilities come in two categories: the ability both to identify and to exploit opportunities better than others do.

In the video-game-console business, the strategies of Microsoft and Sony, which are attempting to dominate next-generation systems, are largely predictable—based on each company's tangible and intangible assets and current market position. Although the core businesses of the two competitors will be affected by video game consoles differently, both sides see them as potential digital hubs replacing some current stand-alone consumer electronic devices, such as DVD players, and interconnecting with high-definition televisions, personal computers, MP3 players, digital cameras, and so forth.

For Sony, which has valuable businesses in consumer electronics and in audio and video content, it is important to establish the PlayStation as the living-room hub, so that any cannibalization of the company's consumer electronics businesses comes from within. After the recent victory of Sony's Blu-ray standard over Toshiba's HD-DVD, Sony stands to realize a huge payoff in future licensing revenues. The PlayStation, which plays only Blu-ray disks, is thus one of the company's most important vehicles in driving demand for Blu-ray gaming, video, and audio content.

Microsoft has limited hardware and content businesses but dominates personal computers and network software. Establishing the Xbox as the living-room hub would therefore help to protect and extend its software businesses. For Microsoft, it is crucial that the "digital living room" of the future should run on Microsoft software. If an Apple product became the hub of future "iHome" living rooms, Microsoft's software business might suffer.

Sony and Microsoft therefore have different motives for fighting this console battle. Yet the current market positions (existing businesses and economies of scope), tangible assets (patents, cash), and intangible assets (knowledge, brands) of both companies suggest that they will compete aggressively to win. It was predictable that they would produce consoles which, so far, have been far superior technologically to previous systems and interconnect seamlessly with the Internet, computers, and a wide variety of consumer electronics devices. It was also predictable that both companies would price their consoles below cost to establish an installed base in the world's living rooms quickly. The competition to win exclusive access to the best third-party developers' games, as well as consumer mindshare, will also probably continue to be waged more aggressively than it was in previous console generations. For Microsoft and Sony, the resource-based view of strategy helps us to understand that this battle is about far more than dominance in the video game industry and thus to identify the aggressive strategies both are likely to follow.

Nintendo, in contrast, is largely a pure-play video game company and thus an asymmetric competitor to Microsoft and Sony. The resource-based view of strategy explains why Nintendo's latest console, the Wii, focuses primarily on the game-playing experience and isn't positioned as a digital hub for living rooms. The Wii's most innovative feature is therefore a new, easy-to-use controller appealing to new and hardcore gamers alike. The Wii has few of the expensive digital-hub features built into the rival consoles and thus made its debut with a lower retail price.

Applying the resource-based view of strategy to competitors in a rigorous, systematic, and fact-based way can help you identify the options they will probably consider for any strategic issue. But if you want to gain better insight into which of those options your competitors are likeliest to choose, you have to move beyond a general analysis of their communications, behavior, assets, and capabilities and also think about the personal perceptions and incentives of their decision makers.

Think like your competitor's decision makers
Since the objectives of corporate decision makers rarely align completely with corporate objectives, companies often act in ways that seem inconsistent with their stated strategic intentions or with the unbiased assessments of outsiders about the best paths for them to follow. So if you want to predict the next moves of a competitor, you must often consider the preferences and incentives of its decision makers.

The key to getting inside the head of a competitor making any decision is first identifying who is most likely to make it and then figuring out how the objectives and incentives of that person or group may influence the competitor's actions. In most companies, owners and top managers make divestment decisions, for example. Strategic pricing and service decisions are often made, within broad corporate guidelines, by frontline sales personnel and managers.

Owners and other important stakeholders

The objectives of the person or group with a controlling interest in your competitor probably have a major influence on its strategy. Sometimes, personal preferences are particularly relevant: it's likely that Virgin's pioneering foray into the commercial space travel industry partially reflects the adventurous tastes of its charismatic founder, Sir Richard Branson. For family-owned or -controlled businesses—public or private—family values, history, and relationships may drive strategy. A competitor owned by a private-equity firm is likely to focus on near-term performance improvements to generate cash and make the company more attractive to buyers. While every private-equity firm is different, you can often forecast the tactics any given one will take by studying its history, since many such firms often repeat their successful strategies.

Other stakeholders may also profoundly influence a company's strategy, so it often pays to get inside their heads as well. You can't evaluate any large strategic moves GM or Ford might make without considering the interests of the United Auto Workers and how those interests might check or facilitate such moves. The importance of nonowner stakeholders in driving a company's strategy varies by country of origin too. If you compete with a Chinese company, the Chinese government is often a critical stakeholder. In Europe, environmental organizations and other nongovernmental stakeholders exert more power over corporate decision making than they do in the United States.

Top-level management

Since the owners of companies hire top-level management to pursue the owners' strategic objectives, a Martian might think that management's decisions reflect those interests. Earthlings know that this may or may not be true. That's why you must study your competitor's top team.

First, that analysis provides another source of insight into the objectives of the company's owners. When James McNerney arrived at 3M in 2001, for instance, he brought along his belief in GE's "operating system," a centralized change-management methodology that inspired GE's successful approach to Six Sigma, globalization, and e-Business. If you were a 3M competitor, McNerney's history suggested that he would try to turn 3M, which had traditionally favored a fairly loose style of experimentation, into a more operationally accountable company. His hiring signaled the 3M board's intention to focus more aggressively than before on costs and quality. It surely came as no surprise to 3M's board or to the company's competitors that one of McNerney's first strategic moves was to launch a corporate Six Sigma program.

And of course, senior executives aren't always perfect "agents" for a company's owners, whose personal interests and incentives may differ from theirs. Such agency problems quite commonly bedevil even companies with the best governance practices, so it often pays to focus on the objectives of senior leaders as well.

Recommended reading

The works below help readers learn more about the ideas and procedures discussed in this article.

The objectives of organizations
Jay Barney, "Firm resources and sustained competitive advantage," *Journal of Management*, 1991, Volume 17, Number 1, pp. 99–120.

David J. Collis and Cynthia A. Montgomery, "Competing on resources: Strategy in the 1990s," *Harvard Business Review*, July 1995, Volume 73, Number 4, pp. 119–28.

Kevin P. Coyne, Stephen J. D. Hall, and Patricia Gorman Clifford, "Is your core competence a mirage?" mckinseyquarterly.com, February 1997.

James G. March, "Exploration and exploitation in organizational learning," *Organization Science*, 1991, Volume 2, Number 1, pp. 71–87.

The objectives of decision makers
Michael Jensen and Kevin J. Murphy, "CEO incentives: It's not how much you pay, but how," *Harvard Business Review*, May 1990, Volume 68, Number 3, pp. 138–53.

Paul Milgrom and John Roberts, *Economics, Organization & Management*, Englewood Cliffs, NJ: Prentice Hall, 1992.

Game theory, scenario planning, and simulations
Hugh G. Courtney, "Games managers should play," mckinseyquarterly.com, June 2001.

Hugh Courtney, *20/20 Foresight: Crafting Strategy in an Uncertain World*, Boston, MA: Harvard Business School Press, 2001.

Anticipating business surprises
Kenneth G. McGee, *Heads Up: How to Anticipate Business Surprises and Seize Opportunities First*, Boston, MA: Harvard Business School Press, 2004.

General managers and frontline employees

Competitors of a decentralized company must focus not only on the objectives of its owner and corporate leaders but also on those of business unit leaders, middle management, and even frontline staff. Until recently, for example, Ford was decentralized, with each geographic region run almost independently. Automotive competitors that wished to predict Ford's behavior would have needed to focus on the statements and actions of each regional and brand manager, because the company's objectives could vary from location to location and across divisions. But since Alan Mullaly took over as CEO in 2006, he has moved to coordinate some decisions and platforms across divisions and regions. Competitors must now understand what is still decided by regional managers and what by Detroit.

For certain decisions, frontline employees and managers are also important, especially if they make pricing, marketing, service, and operational decisions that significantly influence a company's competitive advantage. Even if decision making is more centralized, the incentives of frontline employees may be misaligned with the objectives of a company's owners or senior leaders. Agency problems may inspire the front line to undercut these objectives.

Suppose, for example, that the head of a division at one of your competitors wants its commissioned sales force to promote a new product. If the sales force is enjoying strong sales from established products, reps may hesitate to risk their compensation to promote the new one. A knowledge of such agency problems—which can often be detected through the chatter between your frontline sales force and the customers you share with competitors—can have great strategic importance for your company. In this case, agency problems will probably delay the point when the new product wins significant sales. You could exploit that time lag to fortify your own presence in the market and possibly to preempt the competitor's new offering.

Reach a point of view

What happens once you have a better sense of the options your competitors may consider and the way they may evaluate those options?

Let's say that your company's market environment is relatively stable and that you have much useful information about your main competitors and their decision makers. You can then apply game theory to determine, with considerable confidence, the strategies your competitors will probably follow to maximize their objectives, as well as the way your own choices may influence those strategies. Suppose, however, that even your best efforts don't give you a clear picture of the resources of your competitors or their decision makers' objectives. Then it is often best to avoid trying to predict the competition's exact behavior and instead to use scenario planning to test your company's strategic possibilities.

In a financial crisis, for example, even the best competitive-intelligence efforts may provide incomplete, excessively complex, or inconsistent information on the competition's strategies and thus fail to support game theory or scenario planning. We have found that one way of generating a point of view in such situations is to conduct "war games." In these exercises, each team, representing a specific competitor, receives a fact pack about that company and its decision makers. The teams then make key strategic decisions for the companies they represent. Through several rounds of competition, every team can act on its own strategies and react to the moves of other teams. The war game forces the players to combine incomplete, and perhaps inconsistent, information on competitors to develop a point of view about which moves make the most and least sense for them and are therefore the most and least likely moves for them to make.

No matter how thorough and insightful your analysis may be, two things are almost sure to happen: your competitor will make some moves you considered unlikely, and some of your data will quickly become obsolete. When a competitor acts in unexpected ways, your company has a crucial learning opportunity. Why were you wrong? Did you, say, miss an important agency problem that undermined the execution of the strategy you thought the competitor would follow? Did the market environment change, creating new threats and opportunities for the competitor? Did

EXHIBIT

The competitor-insight loop

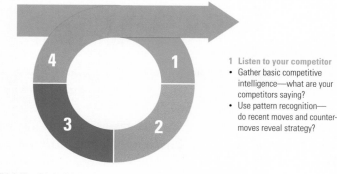

4 **Synthesize, learn, and repeat**
- Synthesize information to a point of view about which moves make the most and least sense for your competitor
- Learn from ongoing indicators and monitoring
- Repeat

1 **Listen to your competitor**
- Gather basic competitive intelligence—what are your competitors saying?
- Use pattern recognition—do recent moves and countermoves reveal strategy?

3 **Think like the decision makers for your competitor**
- Who is the likely decision maker?
- Are the decision makers' interests aligned with those of the company's owners?

2 **Think like a strategist for your competitor**
- What are its assets, capabilities, market positions?
- How might it protect, extend, and leverage them?

it bring in a new chairman or CEO? You must diagnose your mistakes, learn from them, and ensure that you use the latest data to develop your point of view.

Learning from your mistakes means managing these competitive-insight activities as an ongoing process for real-time strategic planning and decision making, not as an annual or biannual event in a bureaucratic planning process. Particularly in dynamic markets, where companies have to make decisions constantly, information about competitors must be updated as soon as possible (exhibit).

One key to making this ongoing process more insightful is tapping into the latest competitive intelligence dispersed throughout the frontline workforce. An e-mail address, a blog, or a shared database could let sales reps report on the latest pricing, promotion, negotiation, and sales tactics that competitors use with key customers or customer segments. Engineers might use such facilities to report the latest product pipeline rumors from professional conferences. When possible, companies should also establish appropriate information-sharing arrangements with key partners; suppliers, for example, may provide the latest intelligence on future input prices. As Ken McGee argues in *Heads Up*, most of the information needed for sound business strategy decisions is already available. You just have to create a process to capture and synthesize it meaningfully.

Related articles on mckinseyquarterly.com

How companies respond to competitors:
A McKinsey Global Survey

How to improve strategic planning

Strategy's strategist: An interview with Richard Rumelt

Particularly today, no company is an island. Those that most accurately perceive the competitive landscape as it is and is likely to be in the future have a distinct competitive advantage. Our process—focusing on changes in the resources, decision-making structures, and compensation systems of competitors—moves beyond the usual updates on key market trends and uncertainties. Its rewards are huge: fewer surprises from competitors and more opportunities to shape markets to your own advantage. *Q*

Hugh Courtney is an alumnus of McKinsey's Washington, DC, office, where **John Horn** is a consultant; **Jayanti Kar** is a consultant in the Toronto office. Copyright © 2009 McKinsey & Company. All rights reserved.

We welcome your comments on this article.
Please send them to quarterly_comments@mckinsey.com.

Google's view on the future of business:
An interview with CEO Eric Schmidt

How the Internet will change the nature of competition, innovation, and company operations.

James Manyika

Few would dispute that Google sits at the center of the Internet. As the leader in search, Google is now the Internet's premier brand and the planet's most potent free service. Managing that commanding position falls largely to seasoned technology executive Eric Schmidt, who in 2001 was tapped for the CEO post by Google founders Sergey Brin and Larry Page.

In Schmidt's years at the company, he has delivered steady growth while expanding Google's reach. By anticipating the ways in which people would expand their use of Internet applications, Schmidt has introduced new products from the popular Web-based e-mail service Gmail (Google Mail in Germany and the United Kingdom) to the recently unveiled G1 mobile phone. And as Google's audience and influence have increased, so too has its appeal among advertisers worldwide.

Making all this happen depends on Google's ability to attract and engage top talent. The organization that Schmidt has helped shape depends on collaborative projects and free flows of information that encourage employees to share ideas. Staffers devote 20 percent of their work time to special projects of their own design, an inventive and effective policy that is at the core of the company's innovation efforts.

Not many executives have a better vantage point on the changing technological landscape than Schmidt. He recently took time out to discuss his views with McKinsey's James Manyika. Schmidt sees more powerful digital assistants arising from cloud computing, markets morphing at an ever faster pace, and plenty of space for human creativity if organizations are willing to carve out a place for it.

The *Quarterly*: *The Internet has radically changed the world. What are the kinds of developments you see ahead?*

Eric Schmidt: When people have infinitely powerful personal devices, connected to infinitely fast networks and servers with lots and lots of content, what will they do? There will be a new kind of application and it will be personal. It will run on the equivalent of your mobile phone. It will know where you are via GPS, and you will use it as your personal and social assistant. It will know who your friends are and when they show up near you. It will remind you of their birthdays. It will entertain you. It will warn you of impending threats and it will keep you up to date. It will use all of that computing power that's in the cloud, as we call it.

Eric Schmidt

Vital statistics
Born April 27, 1955, in Washington, DC

Married

Education
Graduated with BS in electrical engineering in 1976 from Princeton University

Received PhD in computer science in 1982 from the University of California, Berkeley

Career highlights
Google (2001–present)
- CEO (2005–present)
- Chairman (2001–04)

Novell (1997–2001)
- CEO

Sun Microsystems (1983–97)
- Chief technology officer

Fast facts
2007 American Academy of Arts and Sciences Fellow

Chairman of board of directors for New America Foundation; member of board of directors for Apple; member of board of trustees at Princeton

Named one of *PC World*'s 50 Most Important People on the Web, 2007

Informal advisor to US President-elect Barack Obama during 2008 campaign

Visit mckinseyquarterly.com to watch an interactive video of Eric Schmidt.

So, for example, when you go to the store this device helps you decide what to buy at the best price with the best delivery. When you go to school it will help you learn, since this device knows far more than you ever will. So this vision of nearly infinite computing power, network power, and these powerful devices is the basis of the next generation of computing.

The *Quarterly*: *Armed with all this technology, what happens to how people live and work in the world?*

Eric Schmidt: There's such an explosion of content, and yet there's so little understanding of it. So, I think the gap between what computers do—which is very high-volume, analytical and replication work, and the things that humans can do, which are essentially insightful—is a large gap. In our lifetimes, we will not see that gap close very much. Corporations will change the way they sell products to people who are increasingly computer assisted. But ultimately, we still run the world.

The harsh message is that everything will happen much faster. Every product cycle, every information cycle, every bubble will happen faster because of network effects, where everybody is connected and talking to each other. So there's every reason to believe that those who are really stressed out by the rate of change now will be even more stressed out.

However, there's a new generation who are growing up with this as the normal pace of their lives. They will develop the social norms. As leaders, they'll figure out how they want to organize their world, when you and I are sitting around watching them from our retirement.

The *Quarterly*: *Will the Internet bring down barriers, making markets more democratic?*

Eric Schmidt: I would like to tell you that the Internet has created such a level playing field that the long tail[1] is absolutely the place to be—that there's so much differentiation, there's so much diversity, so many new voices. Unfortunately, that's not the case. What really happens is something called a power law, with the property that a small number of things are very highly concentrated, and most other things have relatively little volume. Virtually all of the new network markets follow this law.

So, while the tail is very interesting, the vast majority of revenue remains in the head. And this is a lesson that businesses have to learn. While you can have a long-tail strategy, you better have a head, because that's where all the revenue is.

[1] A phrase coined by Chris Anderson, editor-in-chief of *Wired* magazine, in an October 2004 article of the same name. The theory of the long tail states that as the costs of production and distribution online fall, niche products and services can be as economic as mainstream ones.

And, in fact, it's probable that the Internet will lead to larger blockbusters and more concentration of brands. Which, again, doesn't make sense to most people, because it's a larger distribution medium. But when you get everybody together, they still like to have one superstar. It's no longer a US superstar, it's a global superstar. So that means global brands, global businesses, global sports figures, global celebrities, global scandals, global politicians.

So, we love the long tail, but we make most of our revenue in the head, because of the math of the power law. And you need both, by the way. You need the head and the tail to make the model work.

The *Quarterly*: *So how do companies make money in these markets?*

Eric Schmidt: Free is a better price than cheap. And this simple principle has been lost on many a business person. There are business models that involve free with adjacent revenue sources. And, in fact, free is a viable model with branding [advantages], [charges for] service, and other things. But it's a different business model from what most of us are used to.

A rule of economics is that for manufacturing and mature businesses, eventually the price of the good goes to the marginal cost of its production and distribution. Well, in the digital world, for digital goods, the marginal cost of distribution and manufacture is effectively zero or near zero. So, certainly, for that category of goods, it's reasonable to expect that the free model with ancillary branding and revenue opportunities is probably a very good thing.

The *Quarterly*: *What's an example of how an industry might adapt to these changes?*

Eric Schmidt: Obviously, for things which have some physical cost of production, you'll be losing money in a million units at a time unless you come up with some offsetting revenue. Telephony is a classic example. Most of the costs for telephony physical infrastructure are sunk costs. The cost of operating is not that great—mostly billing and so forth. So you could imagine a situation where telephony went from being billed by the minute to being billed by the purchase of the phone. You buy the phone, and covered in the cost of the phone is a part of that infrastructure. And then you could use the phone forever.

People have to accept that, at least in the digital world, the cost of transmission and distribution is not going to go up. It's on its way down. The people who build physical devices that connect to [transmission and distribution] will eventually morph their models into more of the prepay model, because it will be more consumer efficient.

The *Quarterly*: *What kinds of management changes are needed to cope with all this?*

Eric Schmidt: The old saying is no one knows you're a dog on the Internet, that you can't tell the size of the organization, and so suddenly the Internet levels playing fields in many ways—distribution, branding, money, and access.

But it has a lot of other implications for the way corporations operate. They can't be as controlling. They have to let information out. They have to listen to customers, because customers are talking to them. And if they don't, their competitor will. So there's a long list of reasons why a more transparent company is a better organization.

There are many business models predicated on control. My favorite example is movie distribution windows. As a consumer, I want to watch the movie whenever I want, and on whatever medium I want. But the whole economic structure of the movie business, up until recently, was organized around distribution in a certain format, at a certain price, and then wait a while. But in the new world, people won't wait. A good example was the delay of the *Harry Potter* movie. The fans were fanatical, writing letters and calling private cell phones to overturn the delay. The industry has a fan base that they need to spend time thinking about.

*'Free is a better price than cheap; this **simple principle** has been lost on many a business person'*

There's a lot of evidence that groups make better decisions than individuals. Especially when the groups are selected to be among the smartest and most interesting people. The wisdom of crowds argument is that you can operate a company by consensus, which is indeed how Google operates.

The *Quarterly*: *So, how do you do it?*

Eric Schmidt: You need two things. You have to have somebody who enforces a deadline. In a corporation the role of a leader is often not to force the outcome, but to force execution. Literally, by having a deadline. Either by having a real crisis or creating a crisis. And a good managerial strategy is, "Let's create a crisis this week to get everybody through this knot hole."

And the second thing is that you have to have dissent. If you don't have dissent then you have a king. And the new model of governance is very much counter to that. What I try to do in meetings is to find the people who have not spoken, who often are the ones who are afraid to speak out but have a dissenting opinion. I get them to say what they really think, and that promotes discussion, and the right thing happens. So open models, beyond input from outside, also have to be inside the corporation.

Encouraging this is an art, not a science. Because in traditional companies, the big offices, the corner offices, the regal bathrooms, and everybody dressed up in suits cause people to be afraid to speak out. But the best ideas typically don't come from executives. And, unfortunately, the executives don't agree with me on that.

The *Quarterly*: *What types of people will succeed in this environment?*

Eric Schmidt: I would venture to say that [in some organizations], many people still show up at 9:00 and leave at 5:30 with a half an hour break. And their productivity is defined by how much they can get done in the eight hours. And I would venture today that things haven't changed very much in 50 years. A counter example would be people who are trying to make money in the blogosphere. Bloggers, for example, can't sleep. It's so competitive that if they go to sleep, and a story breaks, all the clicks from their blog go to the others. So bloggers end up sort of disasters on a human scale because they can't deal with the fact that they can't even sleep, it's such a tense environment.

The breadth of information available through Google is not only its strength but also its challenge for users. Read "A user-friendly approach to better Google searches" on mckinseyquarterly.com for a few easy tools and tips.

There's a spectrum in between, and, as an executive you have to think about where you are in that spectrum—both personally and as an organization. For senior executives, it's probably the case that balance is no longer possible. I would love to have balance in my life, except that the world is a global stage, and when I'm sleeping, there's a crisis in some country, and I still haven't figured out how not to sleep. So the fact is that you're going to select executives who like the rush of the intensity. They're going to be drawn to the sense of a crisis. The sense of speed. And they are the ones, ultimately, who are going to rise to the top.

The *Quarterly*: *Could you tell us about how Google innovates?*

Eric Schmidt: Innovation always has been driven by a person or a small team that has the luxury of thinking of a new idea and pursuing it. There are no counter examples. It was true 100 years ago and it'll be true for the next 100 years. Innovation is something that comes when you're not under the gun. So it's important that, even if you don't have balance in your life, you have some time for reflection. So that you could say, "Well, maybe I'm not working on the right thing," or, "Maybe I should have this new idea." The creative parts of one's mind are not on schedule.

So, in our case, we try to encourage [innovation] with things like 20 percent time, and the small technology teams, which are undirected. We try to encourage real thinking out of the box. We also try to look for small companies that we can acquire. Because, often, it's small companies that have the great new ideas. They have gotten started with them but can't really complete them.

Google's objective is to be a systematic innovator at scale. Scale means more than one. And innovator means things which really cause you to go, "Wow." And systematic means that we can systemize the approach—we can actually get our groups to innovate. We don't necessarily know this month which one [will succeed]. But we know it's portfolio theory. We have enough groups that a few [innovations] will pop up. And, of course, we also cull the ones that are not very successful. We push them to try to do something different, or retarget—or, in fact, get canceled. Although that's relatively rare.

The *Quarterly*: *Is there a type of organization that has an edge when it comes to fostering innovation?*

Eric Schmidt: Executives always want to simplify their lives. So they have three divisions, and four products, and all the marketing and so on. That may work in some businesses. But, for most businesses, due to the nature of technology, they're going to become more complex. They will have more products and more variance. And it's part of [maintaining a] competitive barrier to have resilient, scalable, differentiated, and global products.

Which means they can't be built by two people anymore. So, in our case, while we recognize that innovation comes from small teams and we organize that way, we also encourage them to talk to each other.

One of the things that we've tried very hard to avoid at Google is the sort of divisional structure and the business unit structure that prevents collaboration across units. It's difficult. So, I understand why people want to build business units, and have their presidents. But by doing that you cut down the informal ties that, in an open culture, drive so much collaboration. If people in the organization understand the values of the company, they should be able to self organize to work on the most interesting problems. And if they haven't, or are not able to do that, you haven't talked to them about what's important. You haven't built a shared value culture.

The *Quarterly*: *What are some of dangers you see as the Internet continues to develop?*

Eric Schmidt: There are a number of initiatives to try to build essentially a global standard for the Net. Given the history of war and global politics, it's highly unlikely that we'll see a single regime, for example, for copyright law, or for what content is appropriate, or for the penalties for inappropriate content, or for all of the issues that people face in the online world. Today, the way we solve this problem is to use per-country domains. So a domain that's per country is seen as different, such as the US domain, which is called dot com.

There are likely to be legal and political challenges to this over the years, and I think the next one will come soon. The Internet has withstood them so far. The most important thing in these situations is to have a large number of lawyers. The reason is that the laws have become so complicated that, to operate globally, every large corporation I know of has to have a lawyer who understands Brazilian law, one who understands Turkish law, and one who understands the European court. In the case of information, and in particular cultural information, there are widespread differences in what's legal and what's not. The Internet [response is] that people are subject to the local laws.

Related articles on mckinseyquarterly.com

The next step in open innovation

Succeeding at open-source innovation: An interview with Mozilla's Mitchell Baker

Building the Web 2.0 Enterprise: McKinsey Global Survey Results

It would be a tragedy if the Internet, because of these issues, became balkanized at a physical level. It would be a tragedy if every country built, sort of, a police state around its Internet. It's much, much better to use other approaches to make sure that what's legal in one country and illegal in another country does not go from the legal country to the illegal country without appropriate supervision. Q

James Manyika is a director in McKinsey's San Francisco office. Copyright © 2009 McKinsey & Company. All rights reserved.

Letters to the editor

Reader comments on "Google's view on the future of business: An interview with CEO Eric Schmidt" from mckinseyquarterly.com.

A reader writes:
I think that Eric is falling into the mundane (or status quo), possibly without realizing it, with his thoughts on what can and cannot happen. Interesting that he is thinking along the lines of what can be done within the existing structure, rather than considering another paradigm shift. Eric and I have both lived through several paradigm shifts—computers, PCs, the Internet, and maybe service-oriented architecture—so I am surprised that he did not mention the idea that something new could change the very basis of our communication or, indeed, our world.

Gerald Neal
Westpac Banking Corporation
Sydney, Australia

A reader writes:
I think this interview is inspiring; I particularly liked the part related to innovation and scale innovation because it sheds some light on the issues facing traditional organizations and shows how traditional and new management cultures could be at odds.

I also found very interesting the legal issues: it is of paramount importance to avoid an Internet closed in "enclaves," defined by political needs, and losing the benefits of a global network. Cultural arrogance and self-sufficient attitudes are two blights to be warded off.

Mario Castellaneta
Via Advisors
Milano, Italy

A reader writes:
I find Mr. Schmidt's messages compelling, even disturbing.

As a hard-working (and often overworked) professional, one issue in particular caught my eye: his comments on the impossibility of work-life balance in the fast-paced global economy of the future.

What really struck me was Mr. Schmidt's quite natural conclusion that, as the competitive environment will not change, corporations will mainly promote and rely upon the executives best suited to this "always on" grind.

I was troubled to learn that the corporations of the future will be run by a bunch of extremely ambitious and single-minded masochists. Call it diligence and dedication, if you wish. Although I am no psychologist, I fear that this combination of traits will be toxic.

I should be grateful to Mr. Schmidt for giving me another reason to value work–life balance as a public and private good. As it is, he has certainly further convinced me of the possible insanity of doing without it altogether.

William Soileau
Sinodetic
Shanghai, China

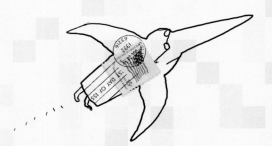

Visit mckinseyquarterly.com for more reader responses to this interview.

Private ownership:
The real source of China's economic miracle

*Even many Western economists think China has discovered its
own road to prosperity, dependent largely on state financing and control.
They are quite wrong.*

Yasheng Huang

The credibility of American-style capitalism was among the earliest
victims of the global financial crisis. With Lehman Brothers barely in its
grave, pundits the world over rushed to perform the last rites for US
economic ideals, including limited government, minimal regulation, and
the free-market allocation of credit. In contemplating alternatives to
the fallen American model, some looked to China, where markets are tightly
regulated and financial institutions controlled by the state. In the aftermath of Wall Street's meltdown, fretted Francis Fukuyama in *Newsweek*,
China's brand of state-led capitalism is "looking more and more attractive." *Washington Post* columnist David Ignatius hailed the global advent
of a Confucian-inspired "new interventionism"; invoking Richard
Nixon's backhanded tribute to John Maynard Keynes, Ignatius declared,
"We are all Chinese now."

But before proclaiming the dawn of a new Chinese Century, leaders and
executives around the world would do well to reconsider the origins
of China's dynamism. The received wisdom on the country's economic
miracle—it was a triumph of technocracy, in which the Communist
Party engineered a gradual transition to the market by relying on state-
controlled businesses—gets all the important details wrong. This standard account holds that entrepreneurship, private-property rights, financial

liberalization, and political reform played only a small role. Yet my research, based on a detailed analysis of the Chinese government's survey data and government documents at the central and local levels, indicates that property rights and private entrepreneurship provided the dominant stimulus for high growth and lower levels of poverty.

We often read that gradualism was the key to China's successful transition from Marx to the market; many accounts laud Beijing for eschewing Russian-style shock therapy in favor of a more pragmatic approach that created a hospitable business environment and allowed private companies to grow organically. This narrative suggests China's economy grew progressively more liberal and market-oriented through reforms that were introduced on a small scale in the 1980s and gathered momentum in the later half of the '90s. Not so. What actually happened is that early local experiments with financial liberalization and private ownership, in the 1980s, generated an initial burst of rural entrepreneurialism. Those earlier gains—not the massive state-led infrastructure investments and urbanization drive of the 1990s—laid the true foundation for the Chinese miracle.

Although many experts contrast China's grand infrastructure projects and gleaming factories built using foreign money with India's dilapidated highways and paltry foreign-direct-investment flows, this point of view overstates the contribution of public spending and foreign investment to China's growth. Neither of these forces assumed huge proportions in China until the late 1990s—long after relaxed financial controls and rural entrepreneurship prompted the initial growth surge, during the 1980s.

In that decade, China's economy grew more rapidly than it did in the 1990s and brought better social outcomes: poverty declined, the gap between rich and poor narrowed, and labor's share of GDP—a measure of the way average people benefit from economic growth—rose substantially. From 1978 to 1988, the number of rural people living below China's poverty line fell by more than 150 million. In the 1990s, their number fell by only 60 million, despite almost double-digit increases in GDP growth and massive infrastructural construction. What's more, in the 1980s China's growth was driven far less than it is today by investments as opposed to consumption. In other words, entrepreneurial capitalism, unlike state-led capitalism, not only generated growth but also dispersed its benefits widely. Entrepreneurialism was virtuous as well as vibrant.

Big cities like Beijing, Shanghai, and Shenzhen are routinely extolled in the Western press as vibrant growth centers (exhibit). China's rural areas, if mentioned at all, typically figure as impoverished backwaters. But a close analysis of the economic data reveals that these breathless descriptions of China's modern city skylines have it exactly backward: in fact, the economy was most dynamic in rural China, while heavy-handed government intervention has stifled entrepreneurialism and ownership in the urban centers.

The significance of this last point is impossible to overstate. Indeed, much of the history of Chinese capitalism can be characterized as a struggle between two Chinas: the entrepreneurial, market-driven countryside versus the state-led cities. Whenever and wherever rural China has the upper hand, Chinese capitalism is entrepreneurial, politically independent, and vibrantly competitive. Whenever and wherever urban China dominates, Chinese capitalism tends toward political dependency and state centricity.

Shanghai is the most visible symbol of China's urban development. Its modern skyscrapers, foreign luxury boutiques, and top-ranking GDP per

EXHIBIT

Town and country

Urban and rural centers of entrepreneurship in China

capita make it China's model city—a glittering testament to the success of state-led capitalism. Or is it? By more meaningful measures of economic achievement, Shanghai's rise is far less impressive than that of Wenzhou, an enclave of entrepreneurial capitalism a few hundred miles to the south, in Zhejiang province. In the early 1980s, Wenzhou was known for little more than its struggling farmers. Of five million inhabitants, fewer than 10 percent were classified as urban. Today, Wenzhou is China's most dynamic municipality, teeming with businesses that dominate European garment markets. By contrast, Shanghai, once home to China's earliest industrialists, is now oddly bereft of native entrepreneurs.

Wenzhou's transformation resulted almost entirely from free-market policies. As early as 1982, officials there were experimenting with private lending, liberalized interest rates, cross-regional competition by savings and loans organizations, and lending to private-sector companies. The Wenzhou government also worked to protect the property rights of private entrepreneurs and to make the municipality friendly to business in many other ways.

Does indigenous entrepreneurship make a difference for human welfare? Abundantly. In GDP per capita, Shanghai is almost twice as rich as Zhejiang, where Wenzhou is located (detailed data on Wenzhou are harder to get). But if the measure is household income—the actual spending power of average residents—the two regions are equally prosperous. In 2006, a typical Shanghai resident earned a household income 13 percent higher than that of a typical Zhejiang resident, but in Shanghai the level of unearned income (for example, government benefits) was almost twice as high as in Zhejiang. Earned income was about the same for average residents of the two places. On average, Shanghai residents earned 44 percent less than their counterparts in Zhejiang from operating businesses and 34 percent less from owning assets. The implication: state-led capitalism may lift urban skylines and GDP statistics but not actual living standards.

The contrast is clearer still if you examine the economic profiles of Zhejiang province and its northern neighbor Jiangsu province. The two make for a near-perfect comparison. Their geographic conditions are almost identical: both are coastal, with Jiangsu to the north of Shanghai and Zhejiang to the south. They also have similar business histories: both contributed significantly to the ranks of industrialists and entrepreneurs in prerevolutionary Shanghai. During the postreform years, however, Jiangsu courted foreign investment and benefitted significantly from public-works spending; Zhejiang did not. The results of that difference are startling.

Jiangsu was richer than Zhejiang 20 years ago, but today it is poorer, lagging behind in every significant measure of economic and social welfare. On average, Zhejiang's residents earn significantly more from assets than their northern neighbors do, live in larger houses, and are far more likely to own phones, computers, color televisions, cameras, or cars. They also enjoy lower rates of infant mortality, a longer life expectancy, and higher literacy. Notably, income inequality is far lower in Zhejiang than in Jiangsu. How to account for Zhejiang's greater prosperity? The most compelling explanation is that in Jiangsu, the authorities meddled in the economy and discriminated against local businesses in favor of foreign capital. Officials in Zhejiang granted free rein to indigenous entrepreneurs, allowing them to build larger, more dynamic local supply chains.

The real mystery of China's miracle isn't how the economy grew, but how Western experts got the growth story so wrong. One answer is that outsiders misunderstood the nature of one of China's most basic economic institutions: township and village enterprises, which some of the West's best-known economists have celebrated as the epitome of capitalism with Chinese characteristics—innovative hybrid entities that achieved high growth despite government control. Nobel laureate Joseph Stiglitz, for example, extolled them for offering an ingenious solution to a problem common to economies in transition from socialism to capitalism: asset-stripping by private investors.[1] These enterprises, he argues, are a form of public ownership that prevents plundering while achieving the efficiency of private-sector companies.

> The **real mystery** of China's miracle isn't how the economy grew, but how Western experts got the growth story so wrong

In short, Western economists have often assumed township and village governments own these enterprises. As recently as 2005, Douglass North, another Nobel winner, stated in the *Wall Street Journal* that they "hardly resembled the standard firm of economics."[2] But the evidence suggests otherwise. A policy document issued by the State Council on March 1, 1984, includes the first official Chinese reference to township and village enterprises. It defined them as "enterprises sponsored by townships and villages, the alliance enterprises formed by peasants, other alliance enterprises, and individual enterprises." The term "enterprises sponsored by townships and villages" referred to the collective undertakings townships and villages

[1] Joseph Stiglitz, "The transition from communism to market: A reappraisal after 15 years," European Bank for Reconstruction and Development Annual Meeting, London, 2006.
[2] Douglass C. North, "The Chinese menu (for development)," *Wall Street Journal*, April 7, 2005.

own and run. All the other entities mentioned in the policy document were private businesses: single proprietorships or larger private companies with a number of shareholders—precisely "the standard firm of economics." Official usage of the term "township and village enterprise" has been remarkably consistent: it always includes private businesses as well as those sponsored by governments.

Western economists erred because they assumed the term referred to ownership. But Chinese officials understood it in the geographic sense—businesses located in townships and villages. The records of China's Ministry of Agriculture attest that privately owned and run entities dominated the total pool of these enterprises. During the years from 1985 to 2002, the number of collectively owned ones peaked in 1986 at 1.73 million entities, while the number of private ones soared to more than 20 million, from about 10.5 million. In other words, the increase in the number of these enterprises during the reform era was due entirely to the private sector. By 1990, within the first decade of reform, such private businesses accounted for 50 percent of total employment in town and village enterprises and claimed 58 percent of their after-tax profits.

Related articles on mckinseyquarterly.com

Reassessing China's state-owned enterprises

Meeting the challenges of China's growing cities

The road ahead for capitalism in China

Confusion about the real origins of Chinese growth has clouded foreign perceptions of the emergence of Chinese companies in the international marketplace as well. It is often said China heralds a new business model for global competition, in which state ownership and the judicious use of government financial controls combine to create a unique source of competitiveness. The computer maker Lenovo is often touted as a product of China's unconventional business environment.

But Lenovo owes much of its success to its ability, early on, to establish legal domicile and raise capital in Hong Kong, arguably the world's most free-wheeling market economy. Lenovo got its initial financing from the Chinese Academy of Sciences, in 1984, but thereafter secured all of its significant investment from Hong Kong.[3] In 1988, the company received HK $900,000 (US $116,000) from the Hong Kong–based company China Technology to invest in a joint venture that would enable Lenovo to claim the city as its legal domicile. In 1993, Hong Kong Lenovo went public on the Hong

[3] Qiwen Lu, *China's Leap into the Information Age: Innovation and Organization in the Computer Industry,* New York: Oxford University Press, 2000.

Kong Stock Exchange in a US $12 million IPO. Lenovo is a success story of Hong Kong's market-based financial and legal system, not of China's state-controlled financial system.

As China absorbs the lessons of the Wall Street debacle and prepares itself for a global economic slowdown, the worst thing the country could do would be to embrace the notion that it has discovered a new development formula more effective than free markets. The real lesson of China's economic miracle is that it was actually remarkably conventional—based on private ownership and free-market finance. China's experience offers the world a timely reminder that reforms designed to encourage these forces really work. Q

Yasheng Huang, an associate professor at the MIT Sloan School of Management, teaches political economy and founded and runs MIT's China and India Labs, which aim to help local entrepreneurs improve their managerial skills. This essay is adapted from his book *Capitalism with Chinese Characteristics: Entrepreneurship and the State.*

We welcome your comments on this article.
Please send them to quarterly_comments@mckinsey.com.

Enduring Ideas

Classic McKinsey frameworks that continue to inform management thinking

The industry cost curve

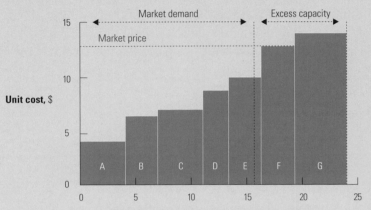

Available industry capacity in order of increasing cost

Each block represents a unit of industry capacity (eg, company, plant, production line); the width of each block represents the amount of capacity available from that unit.

Producers of a commodity are generally willing to supply it as long as the price they can command exceeds the unit cost of production. Yet how do they determine which business units' products can be priced competitively in which market segments? The industry cost curve— a standard microeconomic graph that maps a product's available capacity incrementally in order of increasing cost—is fundamental for analyzing the dynamics of pricing.

Under many conditions, the level of demand for a product and the cost of the next available supplier's capacity determine the market price. In theory, the industry cost curve allows companies to predict the impact that capacity, shifts in demand, and input costs have on market prices. In practice, however, a multitude of questions can muddy the waters. Do competitors have access to a number of markets? Will reinvesting profits in a product shift the market's economics? Does the product's real or perceived value differ among user segments? Faced with such complexities, before the 1980s many businesses relied on a gut-level approach to pricing.

Early in that decade, McKinsey consultants started looking for ways to unravel the complexity. They defined the important variables involved in this curve and the methods for applying it to real-world, competitive markets. Linear programming helped to unscramble a number of options for products, users, and locations, yielding a series of simpler market situations for which the curve can be plotted. By weighing the trade-offs, a company can ground its strategy on the market's predicted price and profit sensitivities, as well as its competitors' actions.

The industry cost curve brings microeconomic rigor to pricing analyses, while still requiring finesse in teasing out the most powerful insights. Ideally suited to commodity products, it is also applicable where quantifiable differences in value exist—for example, the length of time for ocean transits. The cost curve's enduring power is evident in its use in addressing climate change. By plotting the costs of various levers for abating carbon emissions, organizations can identify the most economically viable options.